MAKE

SENSE

MAKE

Architecture
by White

SENSE

White Arkitekter

Published in 2019 by
Laurence King Publishing Ltd
361–373 City Road
London EC1V 1LR

e-mail: enquiries@laurenceking.com
www.laurenceking.com

Reprinted 2019

A catalogue record for this book is available from the British Library.

ISBN 978 1 78627 414 4

Writer and editor: Malin Zimm
Design: Daniel Bjugård

Photography and visuals: Malin Alenius, Anton Almqvist, Aksel Alvarez
Jurguesson, Beauty and the Bit, Måns Berg, Peter Brinch, Ivan Brodey,
Anders Bobert, Citu, Dsearch, Mats Ek, Emil Fagander, Felix Gerlach, Bo
Gyllander, Luke Hayes, Asger Hedegaard Christensen, Thomas Johansson,
Hanns Joosten, Karl-Gustav Jönsson, Per Kårehed, Signe Find Larsen, Bert
Leandersson, Åke E:son Lindman, Henrik Lindvall, Luxigon, Adam Mørk,
Peter Nilsson, Rasmus Norlander, Esben Zøllner Olesen, Patrik Olofsson,
Luc Pagès, Jörgen Pell, Ken Pils, Paul Poinet, Wilhelm Rejnus, Kalle
Sanner, Camilla Svensk, Tom Svilans, Fredrik Sweger, Josefina Söderberg,
Tegmark, The GoDown Arts Centre, Jan Töve, Christina Vildinge, Saskia
Wehler, Hans Wretling, White Arkitekter, White View, White Tengbom
Team, Hendrik Zeitler, Thomas Zaar, Angelica Åkerman

Fact and text contributions: Mark Keiser, Jenny Siira, Margaret Steiner

Translation: Margaret Steiner, Malin Zimm

Printed in China

Laurence King Publishing is committed to ethical and sustainable
production. We are proud participants in The Book Chain Project ®
bookchainproject.com

Preface

Our common values are defined through humanity and culture. Humanity ties people together and makes it possible for us to communicate and achieve. There is an artful expression for every mood and situation in life. Humanities and sciences are intertwined and make us complete. Together they reflect our full capacity as human beings. Of all the humanities, architecture is the ultimate expression of humanist values. I would like to share some of my thoughts on what sets it apart and makes it unique among the fine arts.

Architecture is not possible without positivity. It is always born from hopes and aspirations for the future. It is about improvement. But when we overspend the resources of the planet, lives are claimed among the unborn. We hold the power to limit the damage architecture may cause, and ultimately to save humanity from extinction. Architecture is not possible without collaboration. To build takes many hands and many minds. So many people each hold a piece of the puzzle that make up the result. Being part of such a process has sometimes made me feel small and insignificant. But we all know it: no chain is stronger than its weakest link.

Architecture is not a quick fix. It is slow, probably the most painfully slow art form of them all. A building may take years, sometimes decades to build. A city requires a century, at least. Perhaps the slow pace is meant to remind us that architecture must be more than a statement of today. It will be a part of a future that we know little about. The vision and ideas that we create for our projects need to be strong enough to stand on their own, because they extend so far beyond us. The vision becomes the goal that inspires the project team, the builders, the investors, the politicians and the community; sometimes for years, sometimes for decades, until the project is complete.

Every part of the process counts, from start to completion, and we all know it can be tough at times. This is where passion comes in. When we put passion into what we do, we make a difference on every rainy Tuesday morning. Making sense, and making a difference, is not up to someone else. It is up to every one of us to contribute. A good thing about passion is that it is highly contagious. When we put passion into what we do, we inspire everyone around us. We keep the passion alive through the culture we nurture within our practice: a culture of being courageous and creative, never giving up looking for new solutions. It is in our work culture to be curious about other people. It is a culture of collaboration and knowledge sharing.

Every project starts with a hope for the future, a hope of what it will give to the community, a change for the better. But what kind of future are we striving for? This is not decided by architecture itself; this power lies in the minds and hands of its creators. The 'sense' in 'making sense' relates to both the mind and the hand. We need both sensibility and sensitivity to guide us towards the future.

Alexandra Hagen
Architect and CEO, White Arkitekter

Contents

Introduction

Make Sense is both an imperative and an opportunity. Making sense is our highest aspiration and at the same time the least we should do when designing new spaces for living. White Arkitekter set the sustainable agenda almost 70 years ago and we are still the driving spirit of higher standards of sustainability. It takes curiosity to go beyond given patterns, knowledge to make sense of what you find, and research to structure new learning. That is how we future-proof our projects and make sense through architecture.

The title *Make Sense* was initially the name of our exhibition at Architekturgalerie München (Munich) in spring 2017. By transforming the gallery spaces with different lighting designs, we showed a selection of 80 projects enveloped by the typical nuanced daylight as well as the warm darkness and the filtered forest atmosphere that inspire Scandinavian architects. In order to catch the elusive Nordic light, we envelop

it carefully in our architecture. The walls and roof are like cupped hands, not spilling a drop of light, sculpting its entry gently and allowing its daily route through windows and openings. The number of nuances is as never-ending as the fluctuations of weather and the seasons. We experience the luxury of four distinct seasons; the daylight alters with every time of the day, week, month and year. Daylight is true wealth, to be treasured by architecture. The Northern nights consume some of the daytime hours, transforming the interiors of workplaces and homes into our comfort zones. Scandinavians have an inherent sense of atmospheric lighting, the source of warm and unifying pockets in the sombre hours. Scandinavia is where trees grow old, ideas are young, daylight is pure magic and the natural environment is a sanctuary. We are a handful of nations powered by democracy and litres of coffee, with a soft spot for the middle ground in

↓ The exhibition *Make Sense* showcased architecture by White in a lighting design setting that reflected Nordic daylight.

→ The daylight-filled main space led to an evening light room and then to a video space with a forest feel evoked by green-filtered light, bark and pine saplings. All lighting design by Torbjörn Eliasson.

both rhetoric and mood. This is the origin of White. From this foundation we have built a collective of people who are interested in people: architects side by side with anthropologists, planners next to artists, sustainability experts along with researchers.

White engages in dedicated applied research that supports sustainable ways of life. Research at White is closely connected to our practice and manifested in our assignments. In the same way as our research projects are integrated with our practice, the research presentations are integrated in parallel with the architecture projects in all chapters of this book. Our research provides quality in our projects and involves collaboration between different parts and interests of the practice. White's dedicated practice-based research adds extra dimensions and innovative solutions to our projects.

The development of knowledge has been a fundamental part of our working culture since White was founded in 1951. Our structure of employee ownership allows us to grant support to research and development activities on a broad basis, from bottom-up initiatives in our assignments to practice-based research in collaboration with the academy – all organized and supported by White Research Lab (WRL). Our development and knowledge networks are the spine of our research structure, engaging all staff in the active transfer of knowledge and experience. Furthermore, a substantial number of employees are involved in WRL-funded research initiatives that may run for a week or several years. The independent

research trust ARQ, financed by White, offers further research funding in architecture, urban development and planning, with the objective of linking academic research to practice in interdisciplinary activities and projects. Between WRL and ARQ, White covers funding possibilities for every stage of the research and innovation process, from prototyping in ongoing projects to extensive collaboration with national and international co-funding. By integrating research and practice, we challenge ourselves to take our projects to higher levels of sustainability. Through collaboration between our different disciplines, we find the keys and constraints that make our design relevant and to push our knowledge forwards.

Make Sense presents the result of our practice and research side by side, reflecting the daily work in our studios, where many competencies collaborate to feed a lot of knowledge into every hour of design. The six chapters are divided into types of project that White has engaged in for decades. The first chapter presents a selection of residential projects, most of them apartments, all of them carefully harnessing the valuable daylight, using sensible and sensitive materials and inspiring people to live sustainably. The second chapter focuses on civic life in and between buildings of all scales, from pocket parks to the relocation of the city of Kiruna. It is said that the schools are almost always the biggest workplaces of a nation, counting both students and staff. The third chapter compiles cultural, pedagogical and social public spaces where people meet, grow, create and shape society together. We take great pride in the multifunctional spaces that have proven that one plus one or more functions combined, equals new forms of community where people come together in both expected and most welcome unexpected ways. In the fourth chapter, we are embraced by nature in a journey through a variety of natural environments, filling our senses and challenging us to produce the most respectful architecture in balance with the elements. Chapter five brings us to workplaces that are just as much places that work for people. The final chapter shows how architecture can be a healing force, as exemplified by some of our most warmly appreciated and well-researched projects in healthcare. The chapter titles are imperatives, functioning as short reminders of the long-term perspective of architecture.

We hope to make sense through architecture. People often describe the feeling of making sense as being part of something bigger. At White, we are always part of something bigger.

Malin Zimm
Architect PhD
and Research Strategist at White Arkitekter

Making Sense of Making Sense
Panel Discussion

In order to understand the unique ethos of White Arkitekter, one must go back to the origins of the office. In 1950 Sidney White and Per-Axel Ekholm won a competition for a large social housing development in the Baronbackarna area of Örebro, Sweden. Their scheme had the motto 'You can play in our courtyard' and was designed from an innovative family-centric point of view, its multi-family housing blocks sited conveniently close to schools and businesses. The blocks also had car-free courtyards and kitchen windows that overlooked not only the playgrounds, but also the family bathroom, thereby allowing parents to keep watchful eyes on their children whether they were playing or bathing. Designed from a completely functional and humanistic perspective, this experimental and radical scheme, with its housing blocks grouped around semi-open green spaces and built around a larger central parkland space, was an important milestone in the design of residential buildings. This was White Arkitekter's first project, and since then the office has grown into the largest practice in Scandinavia and the third largest in Europe – with 950 employees spread across 16 offices. Over seven remarkable decades, White has been fully committed to providing buildings and planning schemes that make sense on a variety of levels. Here, White's Alexandra Hagen, CEO, Charlie Bäckstrand, Deputy CEO, and Jonas Runberger, Head of Dsearch, discuss with the design writers Charlotte and Peter Fiell what making sense means to them.

Charlotte: How did that very first project shape the socially based ethos of White? Is it something anyone who's working at White knows of, or is it in the Swedish architectural canon, or is it something that's been consigned to history?

Alexandra: I don't think you can build an ethos on one project, but the design of that housing development was very much a result of our founders' ethos. The ethos of our practice comes from choosing specific kinds of project over a period of time, ones that provide value to the many, rather than just

being exclusive monuments for a few. Charlie, I don't know if you want to add something to that?

Charlie: I think the project, of course, was very much of its time. By this I mean that Swedish society during that period was very focused on those sorts of ethical values. I think, however, that Sid White went further with them. As Alexandra says, it is through the careful selection of what projects we engage in that we have really kept this idea of human-centred architecture at the practice's core. New team members are always shown that first project when they start, but there are so many other project stories in White's history that express the same ethos. You can't say it's just that one, because our ethos is really something that has been built up over the years.

Charlotte: Are there other key projects in White's history that are held up as real landmarks in the evolution of your practice?

Alexandra: There are so many, it's really hard to choose, but I would say there are a number of key projects within residential, masterplanning, educational design and healthcare design that are good exemplars of White's approach.

Jonas: Being educated as an architect in Sweden and then working in practice, all I can say is that White Arkitekter has always been prescient. It's an important part of Swedish architectural history, together with other practices, of course. And because of this, in Sweden, White's buildings are almost ubiquitous in the environment, so it's hard to point out key projects. I think the only way to

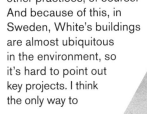

→ Site plan of Baronbackarna in Örebro, one of the most progessive housing projects in Sweden, built between 1953 and 1957. The kitchen was a place in which parents could keep an eye on their children, both inside and outside the house.

understand their significance is to have been inside the practice for a while.

Alexandra: Our former chairman, Magnus Borglund, who had been with the practice since 1974 and was part of the team that put together a recent book on White's history, calculated that the practice has designed enough buildings to be equivalent in size to the fourth largest city in Sweden.

Charlotte: That's amazing! What sort of scale are we talking about in terms of population?

Alexandra: It would be a city of 200,000 inhabitants, so as you can see, White's production over the years has been very, very large.

Peter: You work across many different sectors. Which one do you think you've made the biggest difference in, both historically and in terms of the present day – workplace, or residential, or educational?

Charlie: I would say our impact has been significant in all three areas you mention, because those were the fundamentals of building Sweden's welfare state in the 1950s, 60s and 70s. Those were the areas we started in, but over the years we expanded into other sectors, including cultural institutions. Now we talk a lot about how culture is a driving force in making cities more sustainable, by which I mean not only environmentally sustainable but also economically sustainable. Culture helps make people grow in that sense. That I think is one of White's strengths: the fact that we don't rely on one very specific market area but are actually quite widely spread, in the sense that we are helping to build a society.

Peter: Across those many different sectors you operate in, what is the most challenging? As a non-architect, I would guess it might be healthcare, maybe because the briefs are so constrained. From your experience, what is the most technically difficult area that you work in and why?

Alexandra: One of the most challenging areas is, of course, extremely large and complex healthcare projects. They can be very challenging, but I would say that each market sector has its own challenges. In the residential sector, for example, there is an ongoing debate about how to provide housing that has a good architectural quality but at the same time is affordably priced, so it is reasonable for people to rent. It is a different kind of struggle, but it is equally important, and that puts pressure on us to perform, but in a different way. Of course, if you're looking at technical skills, some of our very large projects stand out. We have infrastructure projects and big cultural buildings that are complex in many ways. We also work on public buildings that are very complex, large-scale projects.

Peter: Are the challenges generally the same from country to country, or do they vary? For example, I can imagine that in Britain right now, residential is one of the major areas of activity. I was very impressed with your Citu development in Leeds [see p.31]. Of course, it's pretty much a planning free-for-all right now in the UK, but developments that are predicated on sustainability are obviously the right way to go, but also perhaps the most challenging. Is it the same in Sweden? Is housing a key area of activity given the population impact of immigration?

Alexandra: It's hard to compare on a global scale, but I'm sure that some of the challenges vis-à-vis providing housing are the same. Many countries are struggling with how to provide good-quality affordable housing to a growing population, but in different ways.

Charlie: I think perhaps the difference is that in Scandinavia over the years we have had the possibility to work in a profound way with sustainability. Sustainability was already very much on the agenda in the 1970s, and for decades there has been an intense environmental discussion in Scandinavia, and especially in Sweden, about how we need to change our way of living and make things in another way. Today, of course, that debate is global. In terms of our own practice, this approach to sustainability started really quite early on, and over the years we have built up a very good understanding of those issues, not only within White but also with our collaborators. You have to interact with the cities you build in, because you can never manage this type of sustainable change as a standalone architectural firm. Meaningful change is achieved by collaborating with a client, or with other partners. That's what we have always been really good at in Scandinavia, and we are now trying to bring this understanding of collaboration outside the Nordic region. For instance, we are starting to work on various projects in the UK. Our success is very much related to how we manage the processes involved with sustainability, but of course we are not the only party in that, it's the cities and the other organizational bodies, too.

Charlotte: Growing from a background of Swedish Modernism, which has been so fundamental to how Swedish design has evolved, did White – during the crisis of conscience in Swedish design in the late 1970s and early 1980s – always stick to the 'Do the right thing' ethos of Modernism? And does it now feel as though people around the world are catching up with the efficacy of your Nordic Modern approach to problem-solving in terms of planning and architecture?

Jonas: For that question you need to bear in mind the Scandinavian context. Different situations determine how practice is conducted. Who the 'actors' are and what role planning monopolies play, and so forth, have a large impact on how architects do things. What developed in Sweden in relation to all these different factors, mirrors, as I understand it, the history of White. Our environmental concerns grew under this umbrella of Swedish Modernism, but also developed from other contexts, too.

I would say that White has a certain uniqueness – mainly because of the number of different competencies within the firm, which have really been a result of the various specialized interests of the partners, but even more than this it is also the way these competencies have been nurtured gradually. It's very hard to say that's a representation of Swedish Modernism, because this rather profound way of working is pretty much unique in Sweden.

Charlotte: White is structured as a collective, which is still quite an unusual thing to find. When was this egalitarian way of working introduced?

Charlie: It was in place right from the beginning, but then it was on a very small scale, because there were just two partners then, Per-Axel Ekholm

and Sid White, so it was two equals right from the start. Then, very soon after that, they denominated two more partners. It was still not a big firm, but Sid White wanted to increase the number of partners. He never wanted there to be one single owner, so over the years the number of partners grew. Then in the 1980s, they decided that it should not just be an ownership of board partners, but that they should also invite other employees to buy shares.

Alexandra: That system of employee ownership has grown over the years; White is well known for it in Sweden. It's always in development and makes the practice a very attractive proposition to any prospective employees. I would say it was a defining feature of White right from the start.

Charlotte: Does it help you to retain good people if they know they have a stake in the company? Presumably it makes people feel more at home in the practice and makes them work harder, because they're working as much for themselves as for the company.

Alexandra: They're also engaged in how the company is run. Jonas, you're an example of a talent that we have 'stolen' from the outside, so why not tell us how it works.

Jonas: From my perspective, one of the effects of this approach is the focus on re-investing profits for development. White is well known for being interested not only in making profit or making architecture that would be noticed, but also in its knowledge production and the contribution this has made outside the firm. In a way we sometimes see our projects as vessels for learning, which was the main reason I was attracted to White in the first place.

Of course, White's bottom-up approach is very much part of this ethos, too, which in practice means that the company's offices and departments work collaboratively, sharing and mixing their expertise and research. And by not dividing up these things into different parts, this means all the employees are actually able to take part in this knowledge development. Then you as an individual also take responsibility for this development, so I would say that owning shares is one thing, but actually taking part and contributing, and being asked to fulfil the expectations you build up, is equally important for job satisfaction.

Charlotte: Do you think of White as having a flat structure? Or should I say, flattish.

Jonas: There's never a completely flat structure. I mean,

Alexandra Hagen
Charlie Bäckstrand
Jonas Runberger

we're sitting here with White's CEO and I'm part of the development team. A company cannot function on completely egalitarian lines because it needs some form of hierarchical structure on a practical management level.

Charlotte: But you do rely on collective consensus more than other firms, or not so much?

Alexandra: I would say that we are actually run more as a democracy than by consensus, because we will never reach a point where all the 900-plus employees agree with everything. So in that sense we are more of a democracy, and that works because the minority always supports the majority's decision. That said, we are always in discussion on how we're going to run the company, but in a way the partners at White are operating with great independence, they can sign quite large contracts without any interference from management, and they then get on and do their business. I think one of the reasons why we have such a great variety of market sectors and of projects is that we allow the partners to develop their business and their projects quite independently.

Charlotte: In terms of how you have evolved as a partnership, it's unlike a lot of other architectural practices that have grown quite a lot in a short time. You haven't looked at a map of the world and said, 'Okay let's put 100 people in Hong Kong, another 100 people in San Francisco', and so on. Instead, you've spread out from your epicentre in Gothenburg across Scandinavia, meaning that you're remarkably Nordic-centric given the size of the firm. I'm just wondering whether that was a conscious decision or something that has grown organically, because maybe you've worked with people in, say, Malmö or wherever, and it made sense then to site an office there?

Charlie: It's been very much in the DNA of White to work this way, and that's because you really need to have a deep understanding of White's culture to bring the company forward. That's meant we've had to grow quite organically. That's at least what we have done so far. It might change in the future, but so far, at least, that way of growing has worked for us. Yes, having partners start new offices has been our modus operandi in Scandinavia over the years, but now, as you know, we have started a new studio in London. It's run by two partners who moved from Stockholm to start the business over there. Our Oslo office was started in the same way and has grown a lot. To start an 'outpost' one needs the people there who have a very close relationship to Scandinavia, because having a good knowledge of Nordic culture really helps one to understand White's ethos.

Charlotte: Are most of the people working at White Scandinavian, or are you increasingly getting graduates from China or wherever working for you?

Alexandra: The diversity of our team is definitely increasing, but we're still mainly Scandinavian. I should add in reflection of our expansion over the years that, especially during the 1980s, we had quite a few mergers and acquisitions. The ones that have been really successful were those where we already had an office in place and we just decided to acquire another business as an add-on. As Charlie always says, it's really important as a company to have your culture in place when you add something new, as you do with any merger.

For instance, the Oslo and London offices were formerly subsidiaries of the Gothenburg and Stockholm offices. By branching out like this, you are not starting completely from scratch, but with a support structure and everything backed up by a bigger entity. So, when people visit our Oslo office, although it's still quite small, they can't help but be aware of the bigger framework behind it. In Oslo, the office is still building its own distinctive regional culture, because as a practice working in a specific place you need to understand the local context and gradually build your own culture to work in harmony with it. The result is that all White's offices have their own character.

Charlotte: Is this something you try to nurture?

Alexandra: The offices look very different from one another, which helps them have their own unique character. For example, we don't have a common design feature for all our offices. So, they are laid out differently and feel distinctive, but the shared central ethos and basic culture are somehow retained [see p.186].

Charlotte: Do they have certain expertise, too?

Alexandra: To some extent they do. Some offices excel in certain areas. Of course, we work a lot across borders and across offices to get the very best team in place for every project, and with the new digital tools it has become easier to work together despite geography.

Charlotte: When you're hiring people, obviously you're going to be looking for bright people with specialisms in certain areas and who have an ability to think for themselves, but are there other personality traits that you're looking for? Are there certain things that would make you say, 'Oh, that's the exact profile match we're looking for at White', or is it very varied?

Charlie: I think what we're seeking in people is actually very varied. We try to ensure that in different groups, we really have a variety of personalities, and we're not just talking different competencies here. We're seeking people who have different ways of looking, different perspectives. This fundamentally comes from your management team, Alexandra, when you're setting up teams to do projects. Having different types of people with different views makes it more fun, more stimulating, than if you were in a situation where everyone thought the same. To get the best results, you need to engage and stimulate the discussion. That's my impression, at least.

Charlotte: What is the median age and also the gender balance at White?

Alexandra: I think the median age is 41.

Charlie: Yes, that's right – but some people are 22 while others are quite a bit older than the average.

Peter: As a median age, 41 sounds pretty good to me, still young but with experience. What's the gender balance, just as a matter of interest?

Alexandra: I think on the senior management level there are a few more women, and the same goes for other management levels too, and I think across the company it is pretty much fifty fifty, I'd say.

Charlotte: That's very interesting. I know that, certainly in tech businesses, women often find themselves in management roles because they have so-called soft skills, which are very, very useful in today's digital world.

Alexandra: I wouldn't necessarily agree about soft skills per se, because you need hard skills, too.

Charlie: I think maybe it's fair to point out that most of the women in management here come from an architectural background or have been in the practice for a long time. In fact, very few have been brought in to be specifically in management. As managers, we've all been part of general practice.

Charlotte: So, they have the technical competence as well as tending to be good communicators, which is the best of both worlds because it means they can manage with technical authority.

Peter: I was reading your research programme document, which is very impressive. How many people are working in that division of your company?

Jonas: There are eight people dedicated to research, working with White Research Lab, but that is just the tip of the iceberg. My own very small Dsearch team that is involved in advanced digital research as it relates to architecture, for example, evolved from that division. But really, research and development is distributed throughout the whole office because it is related to the projects we're working on at any one time. This means that the White Research Lab mainly functions as a

facilitator for more or less anyone in the practice who wants to take part in this type of development work. Of course, the firm's steering committee also strategically plans our programmes of research and works out how best to execute them and which ones to prioritize.

Alexandra: When we're saying eight people, we mean eight individuals who are working at the very highest research level. But when you look at the number of people who are working full or part time within that department, in management and support of research, using the money from our research fund, then I would say you are looking at somewhere between 10 and 20 per cent of the whole company. There are just so many projects that benefit in one way or another from the research and development funds that we have. For example, sometimes I might see something in a project I'm working on which I'd like to investigate further, but the client doesn't want to pay me to do this. So, rather than letting this great opportunity to explore something really interesting slip by, I can apply for funds from our research and development pool, and get the hours needed to do that research in the context of that project. By working in this way, we have a lot of people actively involved in many different aspects of research and development.

Charlie: I think this way of working also creates a challenge because, of course, research and development is something everyone wants to do nowadays. But our office has always been very research-orientated. It's just part of our culture, part of who we are, and our identity. We know our competitors, and what they are doing. But if you have a very strong research organization as we do, it is probably easier to communicate this as it is identified with one's brand. Our research, as Jonas says, is spread, more or less, all over the company, and that is how the research gets truly practice-based.

Depending on the project, it could last a few months or a year, while others might run on for three years or four years, or merge into another larger research project, where many other people will be involved. It's not so easy to tell discrete stories about the research we do, because invariably it's so embedded into the projects we're working on.

Charlotte: Does that research also mean collaboration with academic partners? Do you have special relationships with certain universities?

Jonas: Absolutely; for example, although I head the Dsearch team at White, I'm also a part-time professor at the School of Architecture and Civil Engineering at Chalmers University of Technology in Gothenburg. At White, we have a number of people who have that kind of academic engagement. We also have a number of PhD candidates and doctoral researchers among our colleagues. At White, there's a tradition of conducting research and teaching at different schools, primarily in Sweden – namely Stockholm, Gothenburg, Umeå and Lund. We're also very much engaged in several grander research projects, both nationally and internationally, where academic institutions, research institutes, municipalities and other industry partners are working collaboratively.

Charlotte: Do you get government research grants, say, if you're doing something that's technologically interesting, that might have wider applications? I know in the UK you can get really big grants for doing that sort of thing. Is that something you work with?

Jonas: Yes, definitely. We have a number of funding and co-funding bodies in Sweden. The main ones we work with focus on innovation, and targeting research closer to what the industry is doing. Currently, we have ten active big research projects, but we also have other smaller ones where we're working with, for instance, The Swedish Energy Agency using their funds. Of course, we do a lot of development and research with government bodies that relate to sustainable energy and the use of natural resources, and so on.

Charlie: AI is one technology that we are looking at very carefully, especially with regard to our research into daylight, which is very interesting. That part of our research is obviously related to energy and sustainability, but it's also closely related to architecture. By combining the research work we have already done on lighting with the computational design tools that Jonas and his team are working on, we hope to reduce energy consumption, but also make fantastic architecture. I believe that's what's interesting with having such a strong culture of different research teams coming together and creating something new.

Alexandra: Interestingly, at White's annual meeting where Nell Watson was lecturing about AI and other advanced technology, she said that the building industry is probably, along with mining, the industry that has least adopted all these digital tools. But I think that at White we have always been early adopters of new technology because of our ingrained R&D culture. Personally, I think in the very near future we will see a big shift in our industry, so it's about understanding what our part will be in that, and how our role as a

company and as architects will be affected by all of this new technology coming about.

Jonas, when you joined us at White to start up our Dsearch Studio, you were one of the first to be working on parametric design in Sweden, but that was quite a few years ago. So, certainly parametrics is very much part of our digital toolkit, but we're also working with AI even though it's still in the early stages.

Charlotte: Using parametrics obviously allows you to build and design more efficiently in terms of time and resources and everything else, but do you actually quantify what savings you're getting? Presumably you must be measuring exactly what those tools are doing for you.

Jonas: Yes, we do. I think what is absolutely key for us is the integration of these methodologies. What we're doing is building a framework based on computational development, which we'll need later on for the integration of AI in a way that's appropriate for our practice and for our business. It's not a question of just finding an application to make this happen, but rather of creating a methodology that helps us integrate these new tools in order to enhance performance.

We want to do this from the inside, because the key to the integration is to incorporate all the knowledge and experience that we already have within the firm from different competencies into these processes of simulation and so on. I do have some figures, actually, but these numbers are not solely dependent on the use of smart tools – they're dependent on the whole. The main thing is, the efficiencies provided by these computational tools can only affect the qualities already achieved, otherwise they are pointless. We have examples where wind analysis for instance managed to support key design decisions, which enabled increased areas of terraces with average wind speeds, going from 49 per cent to 70 per cent. We also have examples in the production of our architecture where we can cut down material loss by 20 per cent using algorithmic programmes. Of course, in terms of energy savings we're going for all the certifications we can with our buildings.

We have a big project in which the design is essentially about adding an enclosed covered space in courtyards between residential buildings, where we would be able to change the temperature during the coldest part of the year from a range between −10 and −25 degrees Celsius to plus 12, which would mean that you could suddenly grow avocados in Sweden. All these things are integrated, but the great motivator is the research programme, which hinges on the idea of informed design. That's a very important approach. We introduced the concept of informed design a number of years ago, as opposed to performance-driven design. The main reason for that shift of emphasis is that we use all the capacity of all our teams who are further informed by these computational processes, but are never completely run by them. That's the difference between being driven by something and being informed enough to make better decisions.

Charlie: To add to what Jonas has said about informed design, say from an urban perspective, there's so much involved with this approach. For instance, when we are talking about the planning diversity of a city, it's not only on a social level, it's just as much on an environmental level. If you manage to improve the planning of a city, you will also probably support a more climate-friendly development, because you will have less need for transportation.

Maybe, for instance, you will have more people living close to where they are working, and you'll have more public spaces where people meet. And for those pocket spaces, maybe you'll develop the ecosystem services that will also help create this micro-climate that Jonas was just mentioning. The concept of family can be thought about on all levels, on the housing level, but on a big, urban scale, too.

Charlotte: When you're designing buildings or planning communities, do you think about inevitable change? Because however much you like it, the needs and concerns of society move with the times, so what might be a perfect solution now may be out of date in ten years. Do you even countenance how your buildings or urban planning projects can be repurposed for other things?

Peter: Or made more adaptive?

Jonas: I think this really relates to ideologies of architecture. Someone might answer your question by saying, 'We need to do more generic architecture in response to potential change.' My position, however, would be the exact opposite. We need to design and build more robust,

high-quality architecture.

Alexandra: I think ephemerality is to a large extent countered by creating buildings and urban plans from a 'make sense' perspective, wouldn't you agree, Jonas?

Jonas: I think the perspective I would put forward is not about optimizing architecture for current usage, but about bringing more issues and more values into it. That approach doesn't have to lead to generic and dull architecture, but can actually contribute to making things better and more robust on many levels. From a historical perspective, architecture over time has always been repurposed for other functions – that's just how it is. I think that's an important point to note. Obviously, there are known environmental factors that we have increasingly to consider – climate change and migration especially are things that must be considered now and in the future.

Alexandra: I think one thing that never changes is that architecture that is loved by people always survives. You'll never find a building older than 150 years that is not loved by people, because otherwise it doesn't survive. If a building has that architectural quality, then someone will always make an effort to find a new use for it. I would say great architecture in itself makes a building viable for the future. But for sure you can also, to some extent, plan for the future, and we do that in hospitals, for example. In our plans for hospital complexes we take into consideration future reconstruction of the buildings because we know that the minute a healthcare provider moves into a hospital, they'll start changing it. You can plan for making that process easier, but it always comes with a cost, of course.

Peter: It shows that buildings that are aging well is a sustainable strategy.

Charlie: This is a factor that we think about all the time. Right from the start of any project, we are thinking about its maintenance. What materials do you build with? Are these materials that you can easily maintain, or is it something that will just more or less disappear, and it will not age in that sense? So yes, I fully agree with what you are saying.

Peter: Certainly, there are a lot of steel and glass buildings currently being built that will not age well, and as a consequence will become unloved.

Charlotte: With the increasing use of parametrics and other computational design tools obviously you have algorithms feeding you information, saying, 'This is the most effective way to design something', but do you try to balance that with the formal side of design?

Jonas: Yes, definitely. In my team the four specialists in computational design are all architects. We're working as architects as we develop code, so our focus is not optimization, it's architecture. Bringing in these informed architectural values is part of the process. There are other specialists who come from, let's say, an environmental engineering perspective, but they also have to develop what they are doing in close collaboration with our architects, so the architecture lies at the very heart of the process regardless of scale, from large-scale urban plans to interiors.

Definitely design, in terms of form, is very relevant as well, but there's this potential dichotomy between being rational and an interest in the formal qualities of a building. To me personally, that's not a dichotomy. They're things that can be pushed together, so that when we engage in projects we look for opportunities not only to improve the efficiency of them, but also to add architectural qualities. This involves looking into how things are being produced, what materials are being used, how much of that material is being used, and what might be a better way to produce it.

Charlotte: The psychological aspects of building are presumably becoming increasingly important, too, in terms of research. How do you make people feel comfortable in an environment and give them a definable sense of well-being? Obviously, light must affect that hugely.

Charlie: It's interesting that it's usually not architects in the first instance who are asking that sort of question. It might be White's social anthropologists or someone else out there, talking with people, meeting up, and then bringing in new clients when they are engaging in various communities. We will then come up with an architectural solution in response to these discussions. What I'm trying to get across is that it's not only architects who consider these questions.

Architecture today is very complex, but because we have an interdisciplinary office we can meet the challenge. Our team is made up of people with many different competencies that relate to the psychological aspects of our discipline, and this allows us to approach those communities in new ways.

Alexandra: We like to work with clients whose values align with ours. We would have difficulties, for example, working in countries with bad work conditions and poor regard for human rights.

Architecture is about evoking feelings, making people feel safe, making them feel included, sometimes even making them feel terrified. I mean, all big institutions have big steps that you have to walk up, and really big doors with the door handles very high up, so that you feel small and insignificant just approaching the building. I think architecture at its core is about feelings, while at the same time being a very strong cultural expression. You can't get away from the fact that the shape of a room affects how you feel and how you behave. I mean, why do you get married in a church, where the celing is so high? It's because a room like that is fit for a promise like that.

Charlotte: When you're designing a building, presumably at the front of your mind is the user, or is it the client, or are they one and the same?

Alexandra: Well, the users serve as the client's client.

Charlotte: Yes, that's so true!

Alexandra: If we do something that is not good for the user, we make a bad product for our client.

Charlotte: Does the client sometimes have strongly held, preconceived notions of what they want, when you know that it is definitely not right and that there is a better way of doing things? How do you convince them otherwise?

Alexandra: That's why they need us, architects, because they don't always know what they really want.

Charlotte: Do you choose your clients very carefully?

Charlie: I think it's actually the other way round. Many clients approach us because they know we have a very deep understanding of the client's client, or if you like, the other aspects that are not necessarily part of the brief from the start. In comparison to other practices, we tend to dig a little bit deeper into what the end user needs and desires, and I think that's why quite a few of our clients want to work with us.

Peter: Are you at the point where you can pick and choose your primary clients? Can you turn projects away because you don't like them?

Charlie: We do turn away some projects. There are certain projects, if we're talking on an international level, that we just wouldn't engage in, because they don't fit with our ethos.

Alexandra: We like to work with clients whose values align with our own. We would have difficulties, for example, working in countries that have bad working conditions and poor regard for human rights.

Jonas: We can't get people in our office to work on projects like that. For our partners, our do-the-right-thing ethos runs really deep.

Charlotte: I notice that in terms of your international projects at the moment, you're working on one in Bogotá [see p.228], one in the Republic of Congo [see p.240] and one in Nairobi [see p.116]. Those aren't easy places to be working in, and I'm just wondering if you feel a socio-moral compulsion to be doing these worthwhile projects in places such as these?

Alexandra: The project in Nairobi really springs from the study tours we do each year with all the staff. On one of those trips we went to Nairobi to research the slums there. When we came back from this tour, we felt both that we could have a lot to contribute and also that we would have a lot to learn from this context. We were, of course, also inspired by the engagement aspect of how culture contributes to the formation of a democratic community.

Charlie: It's really all about how we build relationships. In that case it was with a cultural organization called GoDown in Nairobi, which involved working on the ground with these artists and Joy Mboya, who is running it. She had a really fantastic idea about how this cultural centre could serve as a catalyst for development in that part of Nairobi. Of course, because White has a history of philanthropic projects in that region going back to the 1970s, we couldn't resist it.

We said, 'Okay, let's do something here.' Then we started on a pro bono basis, and the project has been driven by the commitment of people within White, who really wanted to be part of it and see it delivered. We are learning so much as an organization just by being part of this project, as we are collaborating not only with the fantastic organization itself, but also with architects in Nairobi, and learning from them how to design habitats in that part of the world. There are so many things that we have then brought back into our other projects.

Alexandra: We are contributing to that society, which is a key aspect of why we got involved in the process.

Charlotte: In terms of the projects you're working on at the moment, or recently built projects, is there one where you would say, 'This is a quintessential White project'? Is there one that perfectly exemplifies your core values, one that represents the essence of White?

Alexandra: It's hard to pick out one, because there are so many ways to be creative, and there are many diverse projects.

Charlie: No, I couldn't pick one either, because the projects are so different in scope, from interior design right up to large-scale urban plans. But saying that, I do have a favourite one – Kastrup Sea Bath [see p.174]. It's the project I always start with when I'm giving a presentation. I always find people are so happy when they are there. They are just enjoying themselves. People walk out there to catch the sun and enjoy the view of Öresund – it's a magical place. To me it's a simple but beautiful building that epitomizes what good architecture is all about, but of course there are many other very good projects that White has been involved with, too.

Charlotte: That's interesting, because when you held your 'Make Sense' exhibition in Germany, you described it as a report on architecture being human. And on your website, a lot of the images you have of the buildings actually have people in them, which is unusual. Most architects' websites show all these wonderful atria that are empty, or buildings with no people in them. I'm just wondering, in terms of that exhibition, what were you trying to say or do? What motivated it?

Alexandra: We were invited and given a free hand to present our work and our office, and we took the opportunity to do this in a comprehensive display of projects.

Charlie: Yes, for some time at White we had wanted to share the discussions we'd been having in the company and invite others to take part in them.

Our colleagues Malin Zimm and Max Zinnecker then started to organize this exhibition, and it turned out to be a very good way of understanding what we are doing, because we are such a huge company, sometimes we hardly know what's going on in other offices. I shouldn't say that, but we just have so many interesting projects running simultaneously. The exhibition was a great way to see them gathered, and that's what prompted this book – because, taken as a whole, it is a serious body of work by anyone's standards.

Charlotte: It's very true that if you have to explain what you're doing to other people, it makes you think more clearly yourself about what you're doing, and that presumably is the process you went through.

Charlie: That's true, but this notion of 'make sense' or 'making sense' was previously used by us in another context. It started as a series of seminars, and was an attempt to take very contemporary themes that are important right now, and try to delve deeper into them in conversation with our colleagues in other practices, in academia, with clients and maybe the public, and so on. The first event looked at architecture and structure from a digital perspective and attempted to make sense of what digitization can bring to us in architecture. For us, exchanging ideas with our colleagues, or even our competitors, is a powerful way of trying to make sense of where we are and how to find better solutions to cope with it.

Peter: There are obviously key methodologies that you use at White. What is the timeline of the processes you use when it comes to undertaking a project? For example, you enter a competition and you win it, or you get a brief – how do you then respond to it? What are the various layers that you go through?

Charlotte: It's a big question, but it's something that no one ever describes.

Peter: Maybe it's too big?

Alexandra: I don't have the one-line answer for that!

Jonas: I'll try to comment on this. There's a wide range of projects, a wide range of partners, a wide range of colleagues here, so there are a lot of different ways of working. In a practice like White, to establish one single process would be pointless, because you couldn't make use of these different ambitions that we have. However, I think the frameworks we have established for sharing knowledge and understanding our research are crucial. There is no formula, but there's a lot of experience, and of course an ambition to share that as well.

Alexandra: One example of how we do things is that we have three very good masterplanning teams, one in Stockholm, one in Gothenburg and one in Malmö, and each has their own approach to tackling masterplanning projects. The interesting discussion comes about when these three teams meet and discuss how they solve

things differently. They do have a network, so they share how they do things, but they each think that their way of doing things is really brilliant and the best. They're aiming for the same great goals, but they have different methods.

Peter: Does every project get that kind of treatment?

Charlie: We always embrace new initiatives because we believe we don't have the ultimate answers. There's not just one thing we believe in, because maybe there's something better coming up. You might merge initiatives or keep them separate. We're open-minded – it's part of our bottom-up attitude, I would say.

Alexandra: No innovation comes from an old process. That's a known fact, so I think our architects continue to struggle between doing things in an efficient way – developing ideas iteratively – and challenging the status quo in order to come up with something completely different.

Charlotte: In terms of the way spaces are now conceived, the importance of informal areas is growing. You see that in workplaces, you see it in schools, and in public environments, too. As architects you must forever be trying to balance introverted cocooning places, where people can be isolated to work on screen doing whatever they need to do, with more extroverted spaces that promote greater person-to-person engagement. Surely, that must be one of the biggest themes in architecture at the moment, trying to build social cohesion in an increasingly digitally atomized world?

Alexandra: I think that's a great challenge ahead. I mean, as we become ever more digital, do we really need specific spaces for specific activities? You don't need to go to the doctor to see the doctor any more. Do you need to go to a clinic? I think the digital arena is very interesting. How is it going to affect our buildings, when we can meet in different ways?

Charlie: We use public spaces for more than moving from one place to another. For example, they are also where we meet and where we relax.

Jonas: I spend a lot of my time in the digital realm, and that's what's driving me personally. The more digital we get, the more difference physical space can make, maybe not in its function in the way we're used to, but on an emotional level. Going back to the example Alexandra gave of getting married in a church: that kind of space is amazing because it has certain qualities that you cannot pinpoint to understand how it functions. You cannot measure it.

We don't need to dedicate spaces to be a clinic or even a library, though we definitely need spaces to occupy that we can put different things in. What remains is, of course, architecture's spatial quality.

Charlie: I also think it is interesting how informal spaces can be used to help find a humane community. How do we create those spaces?

Jonas: I think one needs to create attractors, like a beach, for example. One wants to create attractions that are not specific to one group of people, but accessible to everyone – that have a sense of equality.

Charlotte: In terms of creating a sense of place, that must be something you're always trying to do, because that's what people emotionally connect with. If you do lots of research into the context of a building, for example, do you try to take on board regional aspects, whether it's local materials or regional cultural uses of buildings? There must have to be quite a lot of background research to actually make a building that's appropriate to wherever it is being built in the world.

Jonas: We always talk about contextuality – it's just what we do. But we are also very keen on linking landscape architecture with the built environment. So on most of our projects our architects work very closely with our landscape architects in order to really make a sense of place. It's our daily method of working, I would say.

Peter: One of the biggest challenges in architectural practice today must be the creation of public senses of place when so many communities across Europe are so culturally diverse. How can you create any sensible sense of place or intellectual commonality within a social framework of ever-increasing cultural diversity?

Charlotte: Nature, that's what the commonality is.

In Scandinavia, there's definitely an interest in light because of the very long, dark winters. You have a real appreciation of natural light especially, but also of nature because of the harsh climatic conditions you work with. Presumably, that understanding of nature has helped feed through an ecological awareness that maybe you wouldn't get if you were based in New York or Chicago or somewhere else.

Charlie: It's interesting that you brought this up, because we are currently working in Canada, and we do feel when we talk about light and nature that they are things people over there relate to very much. For instance, when we start talking about the Arctic region, what comes up is how light and the seasons affect our behaviour and attitudes.

Charlotte: In the buildings that you design, do you try to do it so that people can see the changing seasons, because often you can be in a building and you wouldn't know what season it was, because there's no natural light whatsoever. I know of a research project done in England, where a neonatal clinic was designed with lots of windows so that the babies could be exposed to natural light, which gives them a sense of the changing time of day and of the seasons. The better survival outcomes for those little babies are really astonishing, and these are largely because of their exposure to natural light.

Charlie: We have done similar research, not in a children's hospital but in psychiatric clinics. And what we've found is that the surroundings of a clinic are hugely important.

In fact, there has been extensive research into the importance of nature being part of the treatment and, of course, daylight is connected to that. In 2009, we made a publication called *Architecture as Medicine* [*Architecture as Medicine: The Importance of Architecture Treatment Outcomes in Psychiatry* by Stefan Lundin and Lena From, ARQ 2009].

Charlotte: Finally, how do you define 'making sense'? What does it mean to you personally?

Charlie: For me it means always putting people first, but we also need to integrate an understanding of the planet's boundaries into this. It means that there are still limits for all of us. We can't just expand, expand and expand. There are boundaries to manage. But if we manage them intelligently, then, I believe, we make sense.

Jonas: I think it's about understanding the world and sharing that through our practice. That's my perspective, but, of course, no one understands everything. It's a gradual shift, but to make sense of things is to understand them better. And to keep making sense, that's very important. We must never stop making sense.

Alexandra: Very well put, I agree. As things change, we need to respond as appropriately as possible because making sense is everything – it is for White the alpha and the omega of architectural practice.

White Arkitekter stand for beautiful, poetic and sustainable residential architecture, created with insight and empathy. We design for social interaction by introducing shared spaces where people can meet naturally. We aim to improve health and well-being for people as well as for the environment – optimizing daylight and access to green space, using natural and durable materials, and integrating mobility infrastructure for walking and cycling.

By introducing new forms of habitation, we enhance housing and inspire people to live sustainably at every stage of life. We emphasize the importance of neighbourhoods that welcome people undergoing life changes, such as having children or moving into their first apartment. Economically available housing is a global requirement for everyone in a community. Through efficient and appropriate spatial planning, heating and maintenance costs can be greatly reduced. When we work as both developers and architects, we experiment with new architectural solutions and financial models. The core of our architecture is high-quality design, informed by our research into daylight, tectonics, resource efficiency and long-term sustainable solutions.

Acting as both client and developer on some projects has given us an understanding of the need to balance qualitative, yet commercially viable, solutions. We have used this opportunity as a test bed to explore and develop new sustainable options. By increasing the energy and resource efficiency of urban developments, infrastructure and transportation systems, we can design a powerful response to climate change. Our ambition to make sense of residential architecture is to minimize environmental impact and maximize natural well-being – inside, between and around all new homes.

LIVE
AND
LET
LIVE

Koggens Gränd

Malmö, Sweden
Completed 2012

Koggens Gränd is a residential development in the regeneration area of Malmö's western harbour on which White Arkitekter acted as client as well as architects. The 31-unit apartment scheme was an opportunity to push the boundaries of sustainable architecture. Each home is unique and endlessly customizable. Combining the highest architectural and environmental standards, we were able to implement new concepts, energy systems and construction techniques, as well as introducing a new form of tenure, in which individuals actually own their apartments. Buying an apartment in Sweden used to involve purchasing a share in the building, which allowed few options for stable, long-term, customizable home ownership. Koggens Gränd, however, was conceived as purpose-built, owner-occupier apartments that combined sustainable thinking and design innovation while ensuring long-term commercial viability. The apartment layout offers full flexibility, the bathrooms being the only fixed element, thus allowing owners to alter the wall arrangements to suit their particular needs.

It was essential for Koggens Gränd to cope with the harsh coastal climate, while facilitating low running costs and minimal upkeep for homeowners. To this end, the scheme allowed for the testing and implementation of new concepts, energy systems and construction technologies, which were drawn from White Research Lab's experimentation. Materials have been selected with long-life, low-maintenance qualities, with special consideration given to the coastal location. Solar panels connect to the district heating grid through a solar cell bank, while wind turbines (installed on top of the development's multistorey car park), carpools and shared bicycle parking all contribute to renewable on-site energy production. The building is also the largest biogas-generating development in Sweden: organic waste is collected by waste grinders, while separate pipe networks and collection tanks facilitate biogas production. All these features, together with damp-proof construction, good ventilation, open surface water collection and a planted roof terrace, make Koggens Gränd a healthy and pleasant place to live.

← Koggens Gränd apartment block seen from the southeast corner. With White as both architect and developer, a comprehensive environmental approach has been realized in every aspect of the building.

↑ Apartment plan and section.

↓ The metal grid in the entrance to the block is generated as a 'gradient voronoi' perforation pattern by the Dsearch development network at White.

↓ The balconies are clad in Siberian larch, which ages beautifully when exposed to salty winds. The French windows are carefully positioned to ensure the flexibility of the interior plan.

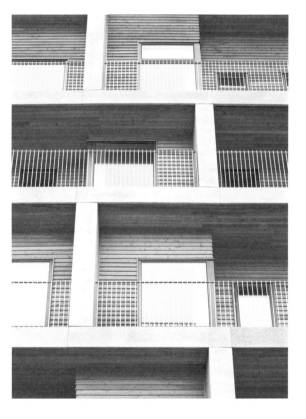

Frodeparken

Uppsala, Sweden
Completed 2013

In one of Uppsala's most attractive locations, between a park and the central station, White has designed a residential building that is a significant producer of energy. Reflecting the academic focus on solar power at Uppsala University, the façade consists of integrated solar cells, making it the largest solar façade of a residential building in the Nordic countries at the time of its completion. The total surface covered by solar panels is 675 square metres, producing nearly 70,000 kWh per year. That is enough to provide all the electricity required for the building's lighting, ventilation and elevators.

The idea to use solar cells on the façade was introduced by White early on, when the city plan was created for the area. The upcoming development of the neighbouring plot was known of at an early stage. The calculations of the power output from the photovoltaic (PV) solar panels could thus account for the possibility of shadows created by new buildings erected in front of the façade. The Frodeparken project was included as a case study in a detailed report about solar energy in urban planning to the International Energy Agency,

where experts from White presented issues, challenges and decision strategies. The issue of 'solar rights' or 'right to light' is becoming increasingly important in urban planning owing to the rapidly growing market for solar energy systems in buildings. The challenge for urban planners and developers is to deal with these cases in a coherent manner over time, as they will certainly occur more frequently.

In 2006 White won the invited architectural competition to design a residential building that combined a high energy-saving profile with distinctive architecture that would help to shape the new image of Uppsala as the fourth largest city in Sweden. The arched front (90 metres wide) faces south to the urban side and the railway station, while the rear of the building faces north and overlooks the park. There are 70 apartments that have between one and five rooms plus a kitchen. Living rooms and kitchens face south, while the bedrooms face north. The ground floor has a glazed frontage and accommodates shops and a kindergarten. On the top floor is a spacious room with a terrace that everyone can use for meetings and parties.

← ↑ The photovoltaic solar panels are integrated into the façade of the Frodeparken residential block.

↓ A shadow study illustrating the sun exposure at noon on a day in February.

→ The façade produces enough energy to power the lighting, ventilation and elevators.

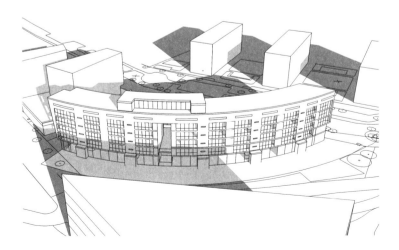

MultiBO:
A new model for student living

White Research Lab 2015

Co-designed with Swedish students, multiBO balances communal and independent living for groups of six students as an alternative to the traditional halls of residence. The starting point for designing a better form of student housing was to ask 2,000 students what they valued most, and the answer was a clear demand for collective housing catering for more than two or three people. In fact, very few dwellings like this exist. That survey was part of a study called Future Student Housing, which was co-authored by Studentbostadsföretagen (a non-profit organization governing student housing standards), Stockholms studentbostäder (the Stockholm Student Housing Foundation) and the architectural practice White, with support from White Research Lab. The survey showed that 35 per cent of the students were keen to live collectively. First-year undergraduates and international students are among those whom multiBO caters for, as it provides a social and support environment that they might need the most. To achieve strong social cohesion, the number of residents in each group is lower than in traditional student dormitories, where 10–12 people often share kitchens and other spaces.

Through consultation with small student work-groups, multiBO was designed on the basis of six people sharing

a two-storey apartment that would have six bedrooms on the top floor, and a kitchen and flexible recreation areas on the lower floor. The central space – a communal living room/dining area – is the heart of the home, a place to eat, chat, mingle and study. The surrounding rooms can be used for individual studies and activities, but connect to the main space with sliding doors. When these are open, the ground floor becomes a generous space for parties and entertaining. Extra-durable materials are needed in the communal areas and kitchen, so stone floors have been laid, demarcating the border between entrance, kitchen and patio. The bedrooms are the students' private spaces, each equipped with a bed and en-suite bathroom with shower, sink and toilet. Space for storage is over and under the bed. This housing solution aims to be affordable for students and to support them in achieving a balanced social life, which makes sense, as people often make friends for life in their first home away from home.

↙ ↓ The central space, shown below from two angles, has double ceiling height. Its surrounding rooms are flexible spaces, as their sliding doors can be closed for privacy or opened to create an even larger collective space.

↓ Plans and illustration for a multiBO solution for a six-bedroom duplex.
Left: Top floor. Right: Shared spaces on the entrance floor, facing the access balcony.

↖ ↑ MultiBO apartment with two bedrooms, private hygiene spaces, a shared kitchen and study spaces.

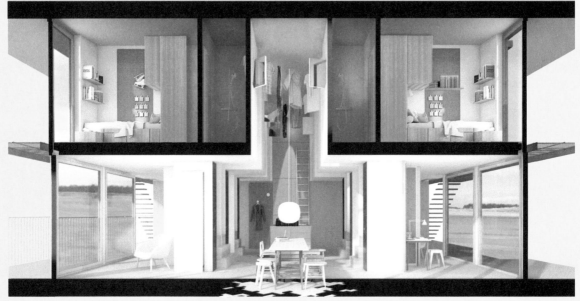

Kvarteret Båtsman

Stockholm, Sweden
Completed 2012

The Båtsman apartments were a central part of the housing exhibition in Annedal in 2012, showing climate-smart and well-planned residential buildings on a typical conversion site, where former industrial workshops give way to forward-looking urban renewal with housing for around 5,000 people. The scheme includes landscaped parks and inner courtyards, water promenades, safe playgrounds and generous common grounds, which make this urban living suitable for young families, who get all the qualities of suburban life, but within cycling distance of central Stockholm.

Each apartment in the Båtsman block has its own individual character, with many options and opportunities to influence how the living area is arranged. Within 75 square metres, for example, the choice of one to six rooms is possible. Even the smallest dwelling boasts a balcony or patio with views of the gardens and the promenade along the water.

Climate Innovation District

Leeds, United Kingdom
Concept design 2016

By increasing the energy and resource efficiency of urban developments, infrastructure and transportation systems, architects can design a powerful response to climate change. Leeds is a case in point. Once home to steel mills and chemical works, today the city focuses on developing healthier, smarter and better connected urban environments for living. The city's Climate Innovation District (CID) turns a central brownfield site into a resilient, green, mixed-use neighbourhood of 516 low-energy homes with integrated amenities for everyday life.

An on-site manufacturing plant, Citu Works (bottom image), will fabricate the timber-frame housing system for all these homes. The plant is capable of producing up to 750 low-carbon homes each year, and is among the

first of its kind in the UK. The Passive House Planning Package (PHPP) has been used at the design stage to assess the performance of the district. From early in the design process, careful interpretation of building information modelling (BIM) meant that the thermal performance of the buildings could be mapped out, ensuring low carbon emissions throughout their lifecycle.

The masterplan converts an industrial area into a walkable, healthy, family-friendly environment. The concept was to build a community based on urban density and an exceptional standard of environmental performance. Housing is fully integrated with services, accessible healthcare and schools, along with offices and the manufacturing plant.

Äppelträdgården

Gothenburg, Sweden
Completed 2011

The architecture of Äppelträdgården (the Apple Orchard) is the result of long-term thinking in quality and economy throughout the planning process, along with the consistent aim of creating a joyful life in and around the houses. Västra Frölunda is a large housing area outside Gothenburg, and is made up of small apartments in high-rise buildings that were constructed during the Million Homes Programme of the 1970s. White was both architect and client in this residential project, which was awarded the highest Swedish environmental building classification.

In order to achieve a more balanced and sustainable population mix, the local authority wanted to diversify the area's housing stock. Providing mixed-tenure family homes means that families with children are given more opportunities to stay in, or move to, this area in Frölunda.

Äppelträdgården consists of 75 apartments divided into terraces of 40 rental units and 35 owner-occupier dwellings across a set of town houses. The 12 apartment buildings, each designed with atria, are accompanied by seven terraced (row) houses with patios. Variations in colour, material and proportion allow the houses to be distinguished from one another and therefore help people to find their way around. In addition, the alleys that separate them have intimate proportions, which facilitate communication between neighbours. The entrances connect to the car-free alley, while the garden windows frame the view of the apple groves.

↓ South-facing façade of a terrace divided into 12 apartments, each of which have a private entrance.

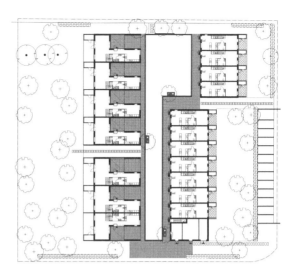

↑ Äppelträdgården provides variation in housing types in an area that was dominated by houses constructed during the 1970s Million Homes Programme.

↑ ↓ On the left-hand side of the street is the entrance façade of the seven atrium houses; on the right are the 12 duplex apartments.

Eyes of Runavik

Runavik, Faroe Islands
Competition proposal 2016

Making minimal impact on the landscape (part of the competition brief) starts with understanding the conditions, accepting them and making the most of them. We therefore decided to make the challenges of the harsh weather and steep slopes of the Faroe Islands into our tools and identity markers. Our proposal for a new residential area in Runavik won the Vertical Challenge award within the Nordic Built Cities Challenge 2016.

The island's stormy weather has historically kept residents indoors and governed what wildlife can survive. The Eyes of Runavik explores historical modes of farming and settlement, where the *hagi* (meadow) is used for summer grazing, and the *bøur* (cultivated land) for growing crops. By adapting these concepts, the new development helps to create a harmonious relationship between nature and human intervention.

The development consists of five three-storey buildings that contain a total of 100 residential units, all built on a steep slope offering vast views over the fjords and the islands. Each building is shaped like an eye and is a self-contained settlement, surrounded by the *hagi* outside and enveloping an inner *bøur* that is sheltered enough for cultivation and social activities.

Each 17,550-square-metre 'eye' structure is built using locally sourced and natural construction materials, such as timber and sheep's wool. Combined with the efficiency of a passive house and renewable energy, this creates conditions for the residences to produce zero emissions over the long term. By adapting to the natural terrain with minimal foundations, almost no blasting or excavation will be necessary, which preserves the natural topology and safeguards the native biodiversity. When viewed from uphill, the planted roofs of each Eye will camouflage them into the contours of the Faroese landscape.

↓ The Eyes of Runavik adapts to the hill terrain with minimal foundations, thus helping to preserve the natural landscape and wildlife.

→ The structure of the development protects against the constant wind, but also opens up to give views over the bay.

↘ Working with the natural slope of the terrain, the Eyes give uninterrupted views in multiple directions.

Future Recycling Centre

White Research Lab 2015

Can we get people to dispose of fewer things? Or, better yet, can we inspire people to reuse and recycle more? Over a period of five days in October 2015, the Future Recycling Centre – commissioned by the city and designed by White in collaboration with the recycling company Ragn-Sells – was tested at the Royal Seaport in Stockholm. The concept, carried out with support from White Research Lab, aimed to define the recycling centre as a social space, rather than a place to dispose of stuff. Using shipping containers as temporary public showrooms, White created a small facility, with sorting stations and a workshop for swapping, repairing, reconstructing and upcycling. At the Future Recycling Centre, an amazing 30 per cent of the stuff to be dumped found new owners, and a further 45 per cent was passed on to aid organizations. In total, 75 per cent of the material originally destined for dumping was recycled, compared to around 35 per cent at a traditional recycling centre.

During the trial period, visitors responded to a questionnaire about recycling habits and ideas, which provided valuable results and insights. Proximity and the ability to leave all disused material in the same place proved to be a key to success. The fact that there were no cars or other traffic within the recycling station contributed to its comfort, cleanliness and safety, which also proved popular with users. The key to minimizing waste, therefore, is in city planning. Knowing where to meet and exchange stuff, and ensuring that things get a second life, makes people happier and brings the local community together. The recycling space should not be hidden away in a windowless basement – it should be a bright and central location for interaction and creativity, with the rent subsidized to facilitate this.

In their practice, architects should first ask what can be recycled in order to create a centre able to cope with it, while also seeking to convey the intrinsic worth and craftsmanship of things. They also need to work with builders to make an inventory of local materials that are worth recycling. In brief, do not let any recycling opportunity go to waste.

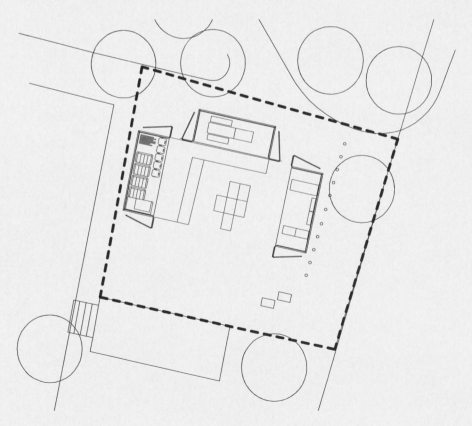

The key to minimizing waste is in the city planning, making sure that people have access to a safe and clean recycling centre. The centre should be an inspiring and central location for interaction and creativity. Left page: Pilot programme plan in Stockholm Royal Seaport.

Friggagatan

Gothenburg, Sweden
Completed 2011

This mixed-use residential scheme takes on challenging environmental conditions to create tranquil living quarters on busy inner-city sites. The Friggagatan apartments are sandwiched between Gothenburg's rail, tram and bus routes on one side, and a busy street on the other. The majority of the 452 apartments are self-contained studios, but these are supplemented by a smaller number of two- and three-room dwellings.

All apartments have a silent side facing an inner courtyard elevated 6 metres above the ground. At street level, the block has 10 units for shops, restaurants and service providers.

By arranging the apartment blocks in five pairs, an acoustic buffer zone was created to protect against the surrounding traffic noise. The residential blocks facing the railway station are eight storeys high, while those facing the street are six storeys. A web of walkways connects the higher and lower blocks at different levels, and these in turn connect to the access balconies and the inner courtyard. The rooftop patio has leafy vegetation and social areas for recreation, including seats for eating and a basketball court. The skewed balconies give the street façades character and provide each apartment with a southward view.

↓ → The walkways that unite the blocks, access balconies and courtyard have mesh panel sides, which make them appear light and unobtrusive.

Dream Home

White Research Lab 2016

The Dream Home project is one result of our research into diverse ways of living, especially in response to new family structures and social settings. It attempted to answer the question: 'What if you need a three-bed apartment one week, and a studio the next?' A wide-ranging inquiry into contemporary needs for flexible living and better use of resources resulted in a development that maximized use of space and minimized use of energy.

The Dream Home can adjust to shifting needs by incorporating moveable walls and careful detailing. The 55-square-metre living space can be subdivided into any combination of one to five rooms, plus the kitchen. In fact, the first Dream Home was built within a six-storey development by making simple adaptations that operate within the structural floor height. For example, the apartment floor is elevated by 40 centimetres to accommodate storage and a bathtub under the floorboards. Some of the structural principles of the Dream Home can even be applied to existing homes, depending on floor-to-ceiling heights.

Research behind the Dream Home has also suggested a new and more accurate way of measuring energy usage: per capita rather than per square metre. Heating and maintenance costs are greatly reduced by efficient and appropriate spatial planning, and the selection of durable materials. Devised in conjunction with the developer Stångåstaden, this new type of housing can cater to the needs of everyone at every stage of life.

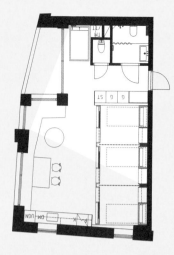

↖ One end of the maximized living-room space, as highlighted on the plan above. All bedrooms are receded into the wall, leaving only shelves and desk space, maximizing communal space.

← Expanded bedrooms, with the beds folded out.

← The 55 square metres of the Dream Home can be arranged as a one-room flat or a four-bedroom apartment. Top: This shows the living-room setting, with bathroom alongside and children in the inset/sunken bath. Bottom: At night, the bed is lowered from the ceiling.

→ The maximized living room has space for a generous dining area.

↘ A smaller seating arrangement, with two of the three bedrooms expanded (camera view highlighted on the plan below).

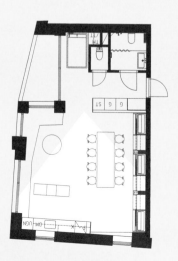

Kvarteret Ankaret

Alingsås, Sweden
Completed 2016

In Alingsås, a town of 25,000 inhabitants close to Gothenburg, a new residential block was built next to the historic industrial area. The three-floor housing project contains rental flats of one or two storeys, and is designed with an angled roofscape that is typical of local architecture. On one side of the development are nineteenth-century industrial buildings that were originally devoted to textile production, while on the other side are low, free-standing residential buildings.

The whole area is embedded in the park alongside Gerdska stream, leading in one direction to the railway station and in the other towards a lake with a popular recreation area. The park area around the new residential buildings was designed as a meadow and preserves the popular stream-side walk shaded by old trees.

Even though each building has the same volume, the roofscape creates variation and breaks down the scale so that no aspect of the development is dominant. Two buildings meet at an angle to define a courtyard that is bounded on the third side by a neighbouring building. This forms a quiet side protected from traffic noise, and opens up towards the park area. Clad in flat redwood panels and with white window frames, Kvarteret Ankaret is reminiscent of the old mill downstream.

The interior of the development is bathed with light. This is thanks to the irregularly placed windows and to the roofs being dotted with skylights, which combine to create a varied and stimulating indoor lightscape.

↓ The characteristic roofscape adds variation to the three-storey row of terraced houses, while the redwood façade harmonizes with old industrial brick buildings across the street.

→ From top, these drawings show the elevation, section and plan of the middle floor of 10 of the apartments.

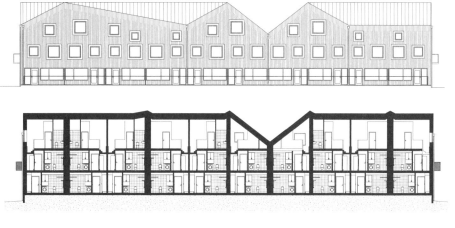

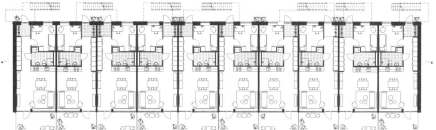

↓ The north façade, with entrances to the two-storey apartments.

Lilla Tellus Masterplan

Stockholm, Sweden
Concept design 2016

The transformation of Telefonplan, one of Stockholm's former industrial quarters, into a new residential district will provide homes for thousands of new residents. The name of the area actually reveals everything about its history: Telefonplan means literally 'telephone square', and comes from the manufacturing site of the telecommunications giant Ericsson, whose head office and auxiliary buildings have dominated the area for decades. The relocation of Sweden's biggest arts and crafts college to this area has attracted young people, who are particularly in need of affordable housing.

In the process of repurposing the existing architecture and developing its potential, White has designed a district that will include six new blocks, more than 10 new buildings, 1,500 housing units, parking for 4,000 bicycles, carpool services, preschool daycare, commercial spaces, cafés and a social centre, the idea being to promote a strong sense of community.

The plan utilizes an integrated mobility strategy, merging public pathways provided for walking, cycling and vehicle transportation as shared surfaces, creating a well-connected and green area.

The Lilla Tellus neighbourhood plan preserves heritage buildings and expands on the principles of the original masterplan. The green public spaces of Responsplan and Radiusparken are both named and designed to reflect the area's telecommunications industrial heritage. These public spaces encourage playfulness and active lifestyles by offering an array of swings, sandpits, basketball hoops, table tennis, climbing walls and trampolines. These facilities are framed by planting based on aesthetic and ecological considerations. Native dawn redwoods, cherry and maple trees, willows and snowberries are planned, as well as seasonal flowerbeds, contributing to air purification and well-being. In addition, buildings are topped by green roofs intended for social activities and outdoor recreation.

↓ The former industrial district Telefonplan is now a residential development devoted to affordable housing. This is partly because of an influx of students, who came when the arts and crafts college was relocated to the empty telephone factory (lower left).

↗ An integrated system of walking and cycling pathways, as seen in this public square, encourages an active lifestyle.

↘ A former office block has been turned into affordable apartments.

A Century of Daylight:
Natural light in residential architecture

White Research Lab 2015

In recent years, the density of cities has increased, while window sizes have decreased as an energy-saving measure. The result is a conflicting relationship between the effort to save energy and the health benefits that daylight provides. White's study of how daylight behaves in five different apartments from various periods shows the dynamic qualities of light and how it is perceived in space. The building volume, street widths, size of grounds, façade materials, room heights, choice of interior materials and shape

of windows are key ways of getting light into a room. Architectural variations over the last century are presented in the image below, which shows the light conditions at the same time of day in the living rooms of five apartments, each typical of the architectural era in which they were built.

The relationship between the buildings and how they are placed topographically has important implications for the availability of light in houses. The Swedish Town Planning Act of 1907 and further

legislation in 1931 regulated the height of buildings and the distance between them. The height was not to exceed the distance between houses constructed in so-called shallow blocks, about 10 metres wide, with 6–8 flats per stairwell. As a result, 1960s town planning saw the traditional town layout replaced with detached, modernistic buildings in the shape of rectangular low- and high-rise blocks of flats.

When the energy crisis hit in 1974, building legislation began to specify smaller-sized windows, but also introduced variation in the height of housing. This allowed better sunlight and daylight conditions, and resulted in an increased feeling of space at ground level. In 2014 it became a legal requirement for all rooms in a house to have a minimum daylight factor level of 1 per cent.

Daylight is a resource; lighting is technology. Daylight provides valuable yet subtle information to the senses, indicating time of day and animating colours, as well as illuminating materials and surface textures, bringing life to architecture. As Nordic architects, we are fully embracing natural light, studying its trajectory, actively inviting its colours and its sensuous qualities, not taking any light for granted, but carefully sculpting buildings to harness it. This is essential because Nordic light conditions vary greatly in intensity and direction during both the daily and yearly cycle.

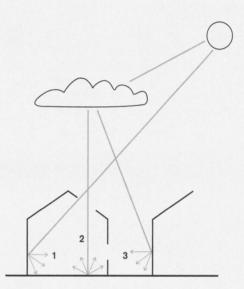

↑ The term 'daylight' incorporates three types of light, which often occur simultaneously within a space: direct sunlight (1), diffused sky light (2) and reflected light (3).

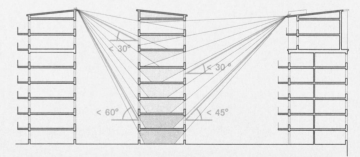

← Five apartment plans where daylight conditions were studied. From top: city apartment block (1920s); shallow block apartment (1940s); high-rise block of flats (1970s); post-modern suburban block (1980s); and a high-density urban block (2010s).

↑ This section shows the proportion of sky that is visible from inside a room. The distance between houses, the room height and the design of windows and balconies all determine the amount of light that reaches the indoor environment.

Slussplan

Malmö, Sweden
Completed 2014

In 2002 White won the competition to design a
12-storey residential building in Slussplan, Malmö.
At the time, Slussplan was an abandoned bus square
in a spot where railway tracks converge and cars speed
by. However, with its location just east of the city centre
and with the canal on its doorstep, the area also had
great possibilities.

The winning proposal provided a new point of
orientation in the city. The building creates a sculptural
landmark, and its compact footprint provided the
opportunity to establish a small public park next to it.
Towards the railway tracks a heavy, dark brick façade
shields the apartments from traffic noise. Towards
the city the building is defined by sweeping balconies
enclosing a wooden façade that will eventually weather
to grey.

The Slussplan building comprises various-sized
apartments of mixed tenure, contributing to the diversity
of the neighbourhood. In this increasingly lively area,
White has also created spaces for commercial use

on the ground floor. The building contains a total of
103 apartments measuring from 39 to 150 square
metres. It also has an inner courtyard that can be
accessed from all the apartments, and a two-storey
terrace with stunning views of the vibrant city, which all
the residents can enjoy. In 2014 the project received
the Malmö Urban Design Award for best residential
building of the year.

↙ 6th floor plan of the building.

↓ Cross section.

→ Slussplan is a 12-storey mixed-tenure
redevelopment between the Old Town of
Malmö and the urban expansion area beyond
the canal.

Overleaf: Three images showing the different
urban conditions around the building:
canalside, railway tracks and streetscape.

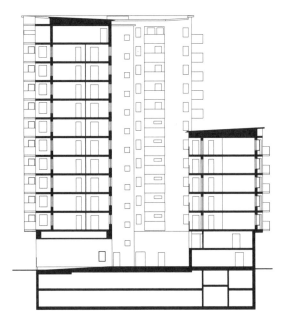

Vävskedsgatan

Gothenburg, Sweden
Completed 2005

In the early years of the twenty-first century, house-building was dominated by a focus on profit, with little or no interest among developers in the construction of rental units. As a reaction against this climate, White initiated an architecture competition within the firm, aiming to encourage and develop innovative concepts that would fulfil the need for high-standard housing on a restricted budget. In collaboration with the builder F. O. Peterson, White acted as both client and architect to implement the winner of the internal concept competition: a 28-flat residential unit with a strong character.

As a result, Vävskedsgatan is far from the stereotype of affordable housing. It is a building of high quality, with simple and robust materials that age well; it harmonizes in scale with its neighbourhood and has an impressively low energy use. The building is 10 metres wide, situated on an elevated narrow site and reaching a total of five storeys. Classic high-quality materials such as hardwood meet 'off-the-shelf' metal grids in a balanced mix.

In our experience from acting as both client and developer on several projects, this type of construction enables good-quality yet commercially driven solutions, but above all it provides a test bed to explore new sustainable solutions. Construction costs for Vävskedsgatan were higher than expected owing to the steep and narrow site and the relatively high number of elevators that had to be installed, but the building cost of around 1,600 euros per square metre was still reasonable, demonstrating that return on investment is possible with small-scale, strong architectural solutions.

↓ The qualities of a challenging site are used as well, as the building leans against the north-facing hill (just visible on the left) and orientates the view towards a stunning open landscape.

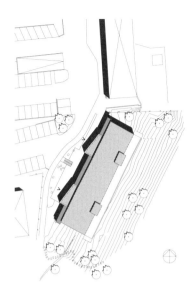

↑ Plans for one small apartment (top left), two larger one-bedroom apartments (top right and bottom right) and a two-bedroom apartment (bottom left).

↓ The balcony runs the length of the façade, giving every apartment a share of the view and a extra space for cultivation and relaxation.

↑ This location plan shows how the building, with the steep hill behind, faces northwest.

↓ A fine metal grid provides a protective frame for the balcony fronts and sides, without obstructing the view.

We love cities for their complexity and diversity. In fact, a city cannot become complex or diverse enough. Good urban design creates inclusive places that address social inequality and mobility barriers, while preserving each area's unique character. We take into account the needs of wide urban demographics, while creating the conditions that bring the city's diverse populations together. By integrating blue and green infrastructure, strengthening connections between and beyond areas, and improving open access to public space, we can design healthy, resilient environments that promote diversity and encourage active citizenship.

Socially sustainable communities are inclusive, secure and resilient – a place for everyone. Architecture and urban design play vital roles in the way our cities and our societies are shaped. We put people in focus to inspire sustainable ways of living; our buildings and environments prioritize well-being, mobility and social cohesion for all. Our architecture brings people together, gets them moving, promotes diversity and creates the conditions that enable people to lead fulfilling lives.

People move to cities to create a better life, to educate themselves, to find a job, to increase their opportunities and become a part of the development. Cities prosper with the influx and mix of people. We believe in the potential of the city as a driver of sustainable development. Public space is an intrinsic part of democratic life and creative dialogues. We aim to empower community on all levels of urban life.

TRANS-
FORM
PUBLIC
SPACE

Kiruna Masterplan

Kiruna, Sweden
New urban development plan 2013

In one of the largest urban transformations of our time, the Arctic city of Kiruna has to move because land deformation from iron ore extraction on its western border will gradually subsume the centre. But how do you move a city while preserving its character and collective memory?

The mining industry is run by the Swedish state-owned company LKAB, and Kiruna is home to the largest underground iron ore mine in the world. A fourth of the municipality's workforce is dependent on the mine, extracting high-grade iron in volumes the equivalent of six Eiffel Towers every 24 hours.

The citizens of Kiruna are taking a prominent role in the strategy for relocation. Inevitably, the period of transformation has evoked feelings of both anticipation and anxiety among the local populace. Through listening to and creating a dialogue with the city's 20,000 inhabitants, the design team works with the people's emotions, ideas and ambitions to inform and shape the strategic plan, thus helping citizens to plan for the future.

In February 2013 White, in conjunction with Ghilardi + Hellsten Arkitekter, won an international competition to carry out Kiruna's phased relocation by 2033. Challenging the original brief, White initiated a 100-year perspective on the masterplan, with the aim of creating a sustainable model city with a diverse economy that is less dependent on the global demand for iron ore. The first phase of the plan is a new civic square, completed in 2018. The first structure to occupy this space (in 2017) was the new town hall designed by Henning Larsen Architects. This was joined by the well-known clock tower, which was moved from the old town hall. By 2021 Kiruna's church will have been carefully relocated to its new site, new schools will be ready for students, and the public swimming pool, library and travel hub will be completed. Extending from the central square and the central axis of Malmvägen will be spoke-like neighbourhoods that will stretch like 'urban fingers' into the surrounding Arctic landscape. The green areas reaching in towards the centre are entryways to nature (see plan, p.58).

Moving the city 3 kilometres to the east while preserving its unique identity is a huge challenge, but also presents an unparalleled opportunity to transform the city into whatever its inhabitants want it to be. The shift is also a chance to create a more vibrant, low-impact and economically diverse urban hub for current and future generations. Focused on a central street, this belt links the heart of Kiruna to nearby settlements, the airport and the mine. Equipped with meeting places and cultural amenities that were previously non-existent, the denser, more intelligent plan promotes public life, broadening the male-dominated demographic of Kiruna's past to allow a more diverse community to settle and thrive. The reuse of materials from demolished buildings and the reconstruction of culturally significant architecture will carry memories while assuming new functions in the relocated town.

Although around 25 per cent of Kiruna's workforce is dependent on the mine for employment, the demographic is changing. In addition to the 3,000 homes that will be relocated, new housing developments will accommodate Kiruna's growing population and the increasing number of tourists. The nearby Icehotel in Jukkasjärvi and its majestic natural surroundings attract visitors from around the world.

The extreme location of Kiruna, 140 kilometres north of the Arctic Circle in Lapland, means that the sun never sets in summer and never rises in winter. The Northern Lights illuminate the winter skies and the Arctic landscape and mountains are within easy reach. With its nearby airport and all the necessary infrastructure to accommodate visitors, Kiruna was an obvious choice of location for the Esrange Space Center, the Swedish Space Corporation's rocket range and research centre. The vast terrain and clear skies are ideal for launching research spacecraft and making observations of the climate and skies.

Through the efficient use of resources, a low-impact development can be achieved in several ways: by harnessing the enormous amounts of waste heat generated by the mining activity, by installing wind turbines to generate energy, and by implementing recycling infrastructure to reduce freight and waste.

The new Kiruna will retain the character of the old city, and be imbued with collective memory. We take pride in our slow strategy and long-term thinking. No one will be left behind and no memories lost while the new city gradually assumes its future position.

↗ Kiruna today. The dotted lines show the demarcation zone, where the land is mined to such an extent that it must be separated from populated areas by a fence.

→ Kiruna in 100 years. The city is moving east as the demarcation zone expands in the west. The zone is divided into a fenced-off zone nearest the mine in the west, and a park area that is accessible to the public but not advisable for holding buildings or infrastructure.

Kiruna today

Kiruna in 100 years

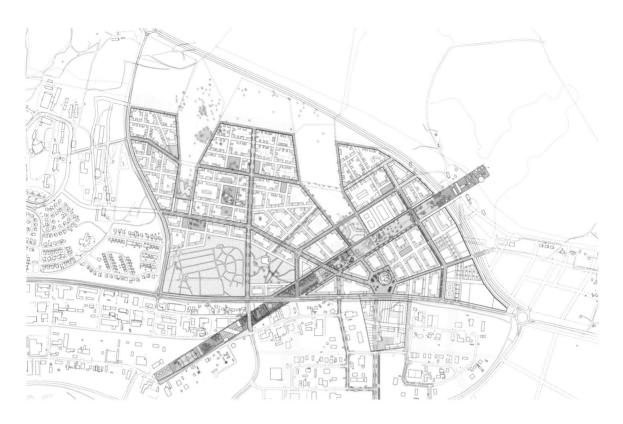

↑ ↓ A series of gradually phased projects will allow the city to migrate eastwards along an urban belt to its new home. Focused on a central street, this belt links central Kiruna to nearby settlements, the airport and the mine.

The first phase of the masterplan is the new civic square (the yellow hexagon above), with completion expected in 2018. The mine (not visible on the drawing) is about 3 kilometres to the west. At the centre of the square sits

the new town hall, Kristallen, designed by Henning Larsen Architects, and Malmvägen is to the south. Alongside the square is the original clock tower preserved from the previous town hall.

↑ Malmvägen is the city's central axis around which individual neighbourhoods stretch out into the surrounding landscape like the spokes of a wheel.

↓ Residents are never far away from city's natural surroundings. The design was created in response to wishes expressed in interviews conducted by White's anthropologist during the competition.

← Skiing and driving snow mobiles are common methods for getting around Kiruna, where snow can fall all year round.

↙ An outdoor pavilion, with a fire to gather around in winter, provides an urban social space that can be used all year round.

↑ Urban vegetation helps keep a comfortable local climate and provide social outdoor spaces for all seasons.

↓ The circular building on the left is the new town hall in this early visualization. It overlooks the public space that will be the new hub of the town.

White Public:
The role of the architect in public building

White Research Lab 2015

As part of a research project to analyse the role of the architect and the role of architecture in public building projects, White Research Lab focused on three projects by White Arkitekter. Each was chosen to represent a particular aspect of social infrastructure: healthcare by the Karolinska University Hospital Solna; education by the mixed-use high school and community house Messingen; and public safety by Park1, a design concept for an emergency services centre in central Stockholm. These buildings were analysed in relation to the role they have in communicating and implementing the underlying political visions of the community.

The socio-historical background of the study is the shift that Swedish society made from production to consumption, particularly during the 1970s. This transformation is visible in the built environment. The first welfare buildings came with the rise of industry and its institutions devoted to education, hygiene and health, and the maintenance of law and order. The architecture of that early industrial era exuded power and dignity, underlining the instructive and authoritative nature of the purpose of these buildings. In the twentieth century, following postwar financial expansion, humanist tradition culminated in the welfare state. Social engineering was manifested in open, light-filled buildings bearing a message of equality and order. Once welfare politics were established, building quality was regulated by extensive governmental regulations. But how is the built environment controlled and regulated in contemporary society? And how are the new goals formulated?

In the deregulated market, the social engineering project is replaced by New Public Management, which requires smart and flexible locations. The individual is the basic unit in the current system, replacing the collective as the political subject; citizens become their own administrators, selecting schools for their children and monitoring their own health. Ideology is less important than economics and safety. The public has not withdrawn completely, but it has changed character. Semi-public meeting places are sought; attractive, dynamic and creative environments are needed for individuals and the private sector, as well as for public collaborations. Both private and public sectors desire an architecture that has an impact on the development of society and creates synergies that in turn generate rent and tax incomes. The analysed projects embody these specific qualities, as well as a generality of function to meet the changing market.

What unites the three analysed examples as carriers of contemporary political values is their spatial flexibility, powerfully executed but not prescribing function. This makes them open and welcoming, adaptable to any programme, with vague boundaries between the activities. Interaction has replaced productivity as the driver of architectural values. The desire for flexibility, openness and interactivity dissolves boundaries within the built structure, which instead is unified by a generous and general entrance hub.

The main role of architecture, according to this study, is to unify all driving forces behind the development of contemporary society, in order to achieve the complex structures that respond to its needs. The collaborative form of the architectural process could set a new standard for many other collaborative processes in society. The role of the architect becomes more that of a process leader equipped with a powerful rhetorical output – namely, architecture. The architectural object becomes a tool for developing the society, manifesting an idea more than a function.

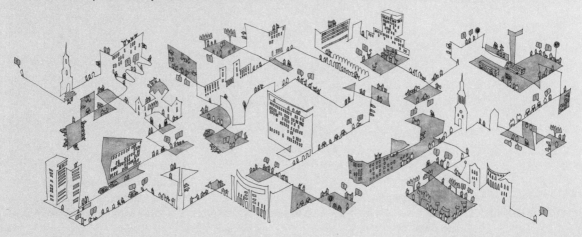

Bee Connected

Gothenburg, Sweden
Completed 2016

Bees are key players in the world's system of eco-services, the benefits provided by ecosystems that contribute to making human life and other life-forms possible. As pollinators of plants, bees carry out innumerable and vital missions that contribute to our well-being. During the Gothenburg Green World festival in the summer of 2016, White, together with landscape architects Mareld and the School of Architecture at Chalmers University of Technology, created a pop-up park to showcase research into eco-services in relation to the built environment, focusing particularly on bees and pollination in urban areas.

As cities become more dense, we need to provide habitats for diverse plants and wildlife so that ecosystems maintain their complex connections, physically and functionally, even in urban areas. This research project investigates the effects of green corridors as one of several strategies to connect vegetation zones and habitats through cities. Green façades and roof gardens are key architectural elements, and complement more accessible park areas and green walks. The pop-up park is designed as hexagonal city blocks that double as plant beds filled with the bees' favourite eat-in and take-away orders.

↑ ↓ In the experimental pop-up park, plant beds are designed like hexagonal 'city blocks' of different heights and filled with healthy treats, such as flowers and plants to attract bees and other pollinating insects.

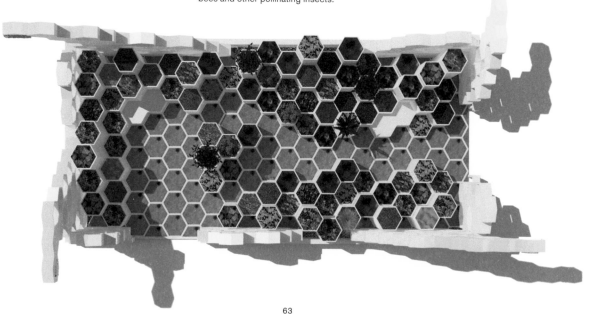

Green Space Factor

ARQ Research Project 2016

Planning how to provide ecosystem services in the urban environment is a constructive way of preparing cities for change. Urban ecosystems respond to the needs of an increasing urban population, maintaining health and comfort, and helping cities adapt to climate change.

Ecosystem services can be defined as the functional aspects of nature that human beings freely benefit from – complex services that stabilize and improve our life conditions and well-being. The services manifest in the interface between people and nature, and demonstrate our dependence on the natural environment in supporting, regulating and sustaining human life and our habitats.

Many previous studies have focused on property space (limited spaces), so the focus of this study on public space is groundbreaking. City planners, sustainability experts and architects at White collaborated to create a tool for incorporating ecosystem services in public spaces at planning level. In doing so, we looked at the impact of connected and continuous ecosystem services in a public space.

One of the results of the research is a planning tool that facilitates the coordination of planning

competencies and integrates ecosystem services in dense urban environments. The integration strategy for ecosystems in dense urban spaces maximizes multifunctionality, so more services are performed by each green space. The tool is a positive feedback system, where credits are awarded to green and blue (land and water) ecosystems; the more multifunctional they are, the higher the score. The ecosystem services included in the tool are biodiversity, noise reduction, surface water management, micro-climate regulation, pollination, shading, recreational value and wellness. A spatial cluster of functions, such as a green space providing shade and relaxation while regulating temperature, improving air quality and absorbing surface water flow, is referred to as an eco-effective surface.

The green space factor is the credit quota of the area of eco-effective surfaces in relation to the total public space surface. The tool therefore not only enables a city planning process to include and potentially maximize ecosystem services, but also allows for their monitoring. The tool is used in a collaborative process that brings together different areas of expertise and enables a creative process that ultimately makes cities more robust and enjoyable. The research project has expanded the green space factor from property to public space, provided a tool for establishing green spaces and giving them the best conditions to perform eco-services, enabled monitoring of the effects, made it possible to identify, increase and connect green spaces, and helped to create attractive and healthy environments for people. As research has shown, material and immaterial values contribute to well-being in cities that have forests, wetlands, green gardens and terraces.

Urban ecosystems provide an array of services in relation to water and land. Furthermore, they are attractive to all living creatures, and help to maintain a climatically balanced environment.

Brovaktarparken

Stockholm, Sweden
Completed 2013

This is a park made for people in motion, designed by landscape architects (nod) C-O-M-B-I-N-E in collaboration with White. It brings an element of surprise to a previously inaccessible and unnoticed underpass. In spite of its exposed and unflattering location, the design emphasizes the experience of motion and offers a pragmatic arrangement for transferring as smoothly as possible from one level to another, whether on wheels or not. The park was created in response to the transformation of the surrounding area from a large industrial site to a more intimate and dense residential area.

Pedestrian and cycle paths, constructed in concrete, wend their way through a system of triangular embankments and terraces, which solve the problem of the sloping site. The terraces, at various levels, are planted with tall pines, wild cherry trees and ground-cover shrubs and perennials. The plants and the public art provide sensory variation over the course of each day and throughout the seasons.

Located under a flyover, the park had to fulfil a number of requirements in the unlikely event that the road overhead might need to be evacuated, or that rescue teams might have to use the park as an access point to it. Having ticked those boxes, Brovaktarparken is an unlikely patch of architectural quality in a difficult site dominated by heavy infrastructure.

↓ The footpath is lit at night, when the aluminium tree, by artist Albin Karlsson, comes to life.

→ Hard surfaces and tough vegetation form a sculptural link between the two levels under the flyover.

Chameleon Cabin

Tjolöholm Castle, Sweden
Completed 2013

This corrugated paper cabin is a little visual wonder, mimicking black marble when viewed from one end, and white marble from the other. The modular construction system is very flexible, and could be extended to any length. A total of 95 components were printed and fitted together using a simple system of tabs and slots.

Based on the proportions of a Swedish *friggebod* (a 15-square-metre shed that requires no planning permission), the cabin was designed to investigate the properties of paper and what the material can achieve in terms of architecture. The project was a cooperative venture between White, the printer Göteborgstryckeriet and the brand agency Happy F&B. This mobile structure has been exhibited in many contexts, such as the architecture biennale in Venice in 2014.

↓ & Overleaf: The corrugated paper cabin changes its appearance depending on the angle from which it is viewed.

→ The geometry and bright yellow of the cabin's interior make a strong contrast to its exterior and the landscape outside.

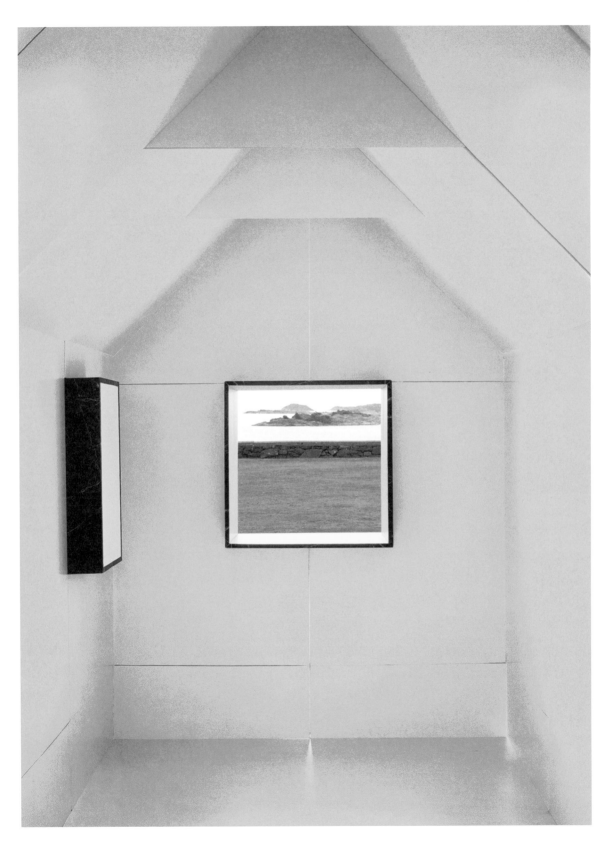

Girls' Room in Public Space

White Research Lab 2016

Decades of research studies have revealed some interesting facts about childhood experience. For example, until the age of 7, boys and girls make equal use of public facilities such as playgrounds. From the age of 8, though, 80 per cent of the users are boys, and that is because girls tend to feel 10 times more insecure in public places. If we aim to create inclusive, innovative and socially sustainable cities, this has to change. Once you have observed the inequalities, you can never go back to spatial blindness.

This project proposes solutions to a problem of inequality that urban planners have been struggling with for decades. The knowledge gap in how to design public places in ways that correspond to young girls' needs and preferences is partly explained by the absence of children, not just girls, in the planning process. A more inclusive process would result in a more equal and multifaceted urban environment.

The project group included architects and social sustainability specialists from White, the Stockholm-based theatre company UngaTur, teenage girls from the youth council of a local municipality, and local teachers. Their first gathering kicked off with a performance featuring two teenage girls interacting within an urban environment that was both constricting and liberating. Local politicians, planners and other stakeholders were invited to the performance and to participate afterwards in a discussion about public places from the girls' perspective. The outcome was revealing. Experienced city planners taking part in the project admitted to never having considered the needs of young girls before. On the other hand, the performance exposed them to the negative experiences of young girls in public spaces, while giving them many constructive ideas that would improve these spaces for everyone, not just girls.

Moving from dialogue to creation during a workshop held at White's office, the teenage participants, supported by architects, had the opportunity to construct 1:50 models to represent a public space by and for girls. The public place chosen was a location that the girls knew well but seldom used. Both project and process revealed their preference for public places with strong character, spaces for interacting in groups of varying size, and places for sitting together face to face while protected from wind and weather. They also expressed a preference for places that integrate information with the public design elements – for example, art installations, viewing screens and mood lighting. The activation of urban surfaces makes it possible for the girls to leave an imprint on their city. In all the workshop models, there was a strong sense of surrounding perspectives and equal attention to walls, floors and ceilings, including their texture and other qualities. According to the girls, the ideal spatial sensation would be like 'entering a big hug'. The models also featured facilities for interactivity and co-creation, and communicated a desire for a stronger presence of art, colour and aesthetic features.

White's collaboration with the girls resulted in a set of references and solutions that were completely novel in the field of urban

planning. This project presents the key qualities we found in this process, including a variation of scale, places offering the opportunity to see without being seen, and spaces providing a sense of intimacy without being constrictive.

What can architecture offer those who experience exclusion? Flickrum explores the urban world from the perspective of a teenage girl. The aim of the project was to develop practical ways of creating 'equal opportunity' architecture by allowing girls to design their ideal public space.

Pallis Pop-up Park

Stockholm, Sweden
Completed 2015

Pallis Pop-up Park was a citizen-driven initiative to create a green oasis, a meeting place and a playground at the sunny end of a street used only as a turning area for cars. Behind the project were White and the Stockholm office of the Swedish Property Federation, their shared goal being to encourage people to take the initiative and bring urban spaces to life. Temporary architecture demonstrates how a city can be democratized and activated by emphasizing meetings and activities that take place free of charge and are open to everyone.

White sees pop-up parks as a way of meeting the demand for green spaces in increasingly dense cities. While this kind of initiative is embraced around the world, and Sweden is no exception, this project in particular prompted the city of Stockholm to adapt new regulations aimed at facilitating citizen-driven city planning. As a direct result of making the Pallis park, the city has made it easier for citizens to influence their environment and engage with the architectural process, and Stockholm City's Traffic Office and the Swedish Property Federation have jointly produced *The Citizen's Handbook of Urban Development*. Highlights include the introduction of new deposits to secure a suitable site, and more flexible ways to rent it. Pop-ups created for minor non-commercial events are eligible for a no-cost permit in order to increase urban cultural amenity. It is also now easier to build temporary parks in parking spaces. Pallis is an example of democratic architecture in action and has actively improved well-being in a densely populated urban environment.

White's concept of a small, or 'pocket', pop-up park focuses on creating healthy spaces, so it emphasizes the importance of biodiversity in strengthening ecosystems. By integrating ecological elements, it creates a micro-climate where flora, fauna and humans can thrive in equal measure (see overleaf). A sustainable living ecosystem within a pocket park means that it can be used to counteract the negative effects of the urban environment. For example, a site as small as 13 x 15 metres can contain green walls that filter the city air, dampen traffic noise and become a habitat for small creatures; surface water ponds that purify rainwater; nesting boxes fixed to lamp-posts to attract birds; and insect homes and beehives to house pollinators. Seed exchanges let visitors take a bit of the park home with them and contribute their own plants in seed swap events. Pocket parks can also host community events, which extend their season to make them year-round places of interest and support local expressions of culture.

The Pallis Pop-up Park put all these concepts into action. For the duration of June 2015, cars were banned from a small section of Stockholm's Södermalm while the community stepped in to design their very own pop-up park. Pallis evolved to include DIY jewellery-making and skateboard deck design workshops, food trucks, DJs and live performances, as well as group tutorials on how to design and implement the horticultural and ecosystem services underpinning the park. At the end of the month, all the components of the park were donated to visitors to be repurposed in their own homes and neighbourhoods.

↑ ↓ ← The site above was turned into Pallis Pop-up Park (below). The initiative was driven by local citizens, who transformed the parking area into a vivid meeting place.

Overleaf: A pocket park design concept that demonstrates how even a small area of 13 x 15 metres can provide substantial ecosystem services and social value.

St Johannesplan

Malmö, Sweden
Completed 2011

When the new City Tunnel station opened at Triangeln in central Malmö, the areas around St Johannesplan and Konsthallstorget transformed from two small, quiet city squares into a transition space for the region's 37,000 commuters. The challenge was to create new urban public spaces that would accommodate commuters during weekday rush hours while also lending themselves to quiet Sunday afternoons. White connected two previously separate sides of the square into one welcoming and functional surface, achieved by the detailing of the uniquely patterned concrete floor. The two major stakeholders in this redevelopment were the council and the Church, and White acted as mediator. Thanks to their cooperation, we managed to erase all visible borders between public and Church-owned areas.

With the focus on sustainable transportation, the new square promotes the needs of pedestrians, cyclists and train commuters over road traffic, which is limited to buses and taxis in clearly marked areas on the connecting stone slabs. There are ample spaces for bicycles and clear paths for walkers. This project is the result of the architect's double role as designer and mediator. When society is rethinking the use of public space, the architect has an important role in supporting the necessary changes that will lead to a sustainable urban future.

↓ At one end of the square is the domed entrance to the new train station and at the other is a circular seating or performance platform (shown here) in smooth concrete with fractal pattern inlays and integrated lighting.

→ Car traffic is minimized to the benefit of cyclists and pedestrians. Swathes of grass pop up like islands in paving, creating another rhythm of motion in the space.

↘ The artist Ebba Matz was an an integral part of the design team, her major contribution being the thorn-shaped pathways leading the way to St Johannes Church (to the left in this image), also known as the 'church of roses'.

Bäckparken

Linköping, Sweden
Completed 2016

Bäckparken was the first project to be implemented in the new urban development of Vallastaden. It pre-dated the construction of residential buildings and literally prepared the ground for growing a new neighbourhood. By beginning the development with the park, the ideal environmental conditions are considered at an early stage. This also means that the habitat is allowed more time to mature and soften the landscape. As new residents of all ages begin populating the park and creating a flow of their own, the attractive brook that runs through it connects the outdoor social spaces with the technical aspects of water purification.

Bäckparken (brook park) was planned by a multi-disciplinary team in collaboration with an ecologist specializing in limnology, the science of flowing water and streams. The ecological system performs complex tasks, most importantly sustaining wildlife both in and out of the water, while the water is purified by its natural flow. Watching the glimmering running water from the wooden footbridge, the fact that the brook is part of a grey-water system may go largely unnoticed, but that is exactly the point.

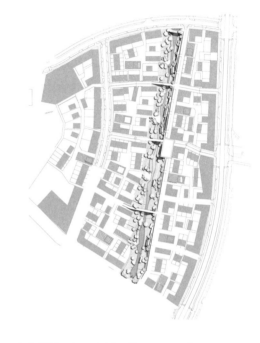

← ↑ Bäckparken stretches like a green and blue spine through the new residential area of Vallastaden.

↓ Robust plants have been chosen for their ability to thrive in water levels that may vary by as much as 1 metre during the course of a day.

Kungsbacka Torg

Kungsbacka, Sweden
Completed 2012

An invisible building is present in the town square of Kungsbacka. If you look carefully at the granite paving, you can see the outline of a church that once stood on the site, a nod towards the town's history. The 'ghost' church is furnished with rows of benches so that people can sit and enjoy the weather, or rest after a night out. Kungsbacka Torg has undergone many changes over the years. After the church fell into ruins, the area became a mundane car park, which for some decades was the fate of many small town squares in Sweden.

This project illustrates the rising interest among small and middle-sized Swedish towns in having an attractive square that functions as an open and social space rather than a car park. Since 2010, after a long period of neglect, this square has been restored to its original function as a public living room.

The ghostly church in Kungsbacka square is a friendly presence, watching over the social life and welcoming everyone to activities and gatherings. The cherry trees along the south side of the square paint this urban living room in the colours of the season.

→ The illumination under the public benches provides a welcoming glow while also contributing to the lighting of the square.

↓ The outline of the church in the middle of Kungsbacka Torg harks back to the town's history and promotes civic pride.

Södra Skanstull Masterplan

Skanstull, Stockholm
Masterplan proposal 2017

The city of Stockholm needs to build 160,000 new homes by 2030. In order to cope with this challenge, the urban environment necessarily becomes more dense, with the consequence that boundaries between the city and adjacent suburbs are reduced. Many areas of the Södra Skanstull district are currently underused, so the new masterplan has two main ambitions: to increase social integration by increasing connectivity, and to promote healthy forms of mobility as part of a wider strategy to create a walkable city.

Södra Skanstull is a multifaceted area in south central Stockholm, with diverse activities, including nature trails, boating and a bustling club scene. Busy road infrastructure and flyovers dominate some parts of the area and yet it is abruptly cut off from city life by the horizontal layering of the site. At the upper levels there is a wealth of commercial and retail activity, giving rise to overcrowded and inefficient public spaces. There are also many barriers to pedestrian mobility, which arise from the differences in level created by the road and bridge infrastructure.

A new green diagonal thoroughfare will connect Ringvägen in the west with the lower quay level to the east, and there will be new public spaces, homes, offices and hotels. Residential blocks are 5–7 floors high, somewhat lower than the two high-rise buildings alongside, which reflect the tower heights of two nearby commercial properties. In the south, new sports and leisure amenities supplement the outdoor and indoor swimming pools of the 1920s Eriksdalsbadet swimming centre, along with gyms and badminton

courts. Existing cultural establishments, such as the popular Trädgården Club under the bridges, are left untouched. Part of the strategy for social integration is new connections between schools, parks and leisure activities, designed to complement the busy public transport-nodes in Skanstull.

Residents and local stakeholders value different aspects of the site, depending on their location and circumstances, but they have played a vital role in the design process to date, and will continue to influence the shaping of their neighbourhood. The masterplan aims at enhancing the identity of the area by preserving certain existing features, such as Eriksdalsbadet Swimming Pool, popular sports facilities and allotments. Nonetheless, the boundaries and identity of Södra Skanstull are vague. To improve this, the masterplan provides a new central hub, with 65,000 square metres allocated to culture, sport and offices, 22,000 square metres to commerce, and 750 new apartments. The proposal also introduces new structures to minimize traffic noise and pollution. Phased construction will commence in 2019.

By reappraising the in-between spaces of the dominating road infrastructure, the masterplan shows that underused spaces can be rejuvenated for urban life and promote walking and biking.

↓ The masterplan includes 750 new homes, plus offices, hotels and culture and sports facilities, as well as connecting both sides of the Skanstull bridge.

↑ A central street cuts diagonally through the new blocks, connecting the upper street level with the bankside level, encouraging locals to cycle and walk.

↓ The plan for Södra Skanstull aims to create a safe and well-connected city neighbourhood, even when working within the limitations imposed by old infrastructure.

Stadsberget

Piteå, Sweden
Completed 2015

Located in the town of Piteå, about 130 kilometres below the Arctic Circle, Stadsberget – the City Mountain – is a five-storey parking garage. However, the building's other functions are why it is the talk of the town. Designed with the idea of enjoying live music in the warmth of the summer sun, the slope is a viewpoint, a meeting place, an amphitheatre and a tobogganing hill, depending on season, light and weather conditions.

Its façades are clad with larch wood in a composition of undulating shapes, and floodlighting – programmed to follow the seasons – is seamlessly integrated into the façade design. During the darkest five months of the year, the building glows like a lantern. The bottom of the slope provides Piteå with a small town square connecting the northern and southern districts of the city.

↓ The building has a sophisticated lighting programme, which allows it to be illuminated like a lantern in the evening, while exuding a natural warm glow during the day.

→ In a nod to Piteå's reputation for forestry and related crafts, wood is, unsurprisingly, the dominant building material for the Stadsberget. The entire façade is clad in larch battens, all mounted with great precision.

↘ The slope on one side of the car park acts as a playground, where children can toboggan to their hearts' content.

The Forumtorget Bench

White Research Lab 2016

Public space is shared by everyone, so it must be adapted to general rather than individual needs. While this rule often leads to generic design following standard dimensions, the 60-metre Forumtorget bench was created to manifest diversity in the ways we may take a seat in the public domain. Based on a rational logic for design, fabrication and construction, the bench takes its form from the diverse shapes of the human body. As you move along the length of the bench, the seating height and depth, backrest inclination and overall dimensions transform so that each person can find a favourite, almost tailor-made spot. The bench is the collective form of hundreds of individual chairs, an alternative way of creating public seating in an urban context, and in this particular site, negotiating a sloping square with differing heights along its stretch.

The development of this site-specific furniture was conducted by an interdisciplinary team coordinated by the development network Dsearch, using a computational design system that could handle the complexity. This approach allowed more time to be spent on the investigation of good seating parameters, appropriate materials and details for construction, leaving the final decision about the actual form to the very end. This mode of working allowed a strong combination of intuitive design thinking, material

investigations and performance criteria to be combined into the process, and the final form came through the aid of direct digital transfer from the design model to the digital production process.

The bench was produced in quartz composite and glass, cut to shape using water-jet technology, then combined into modules on a steel undercarriage, and placed on a concrete foundation in situ. It incorporates an adaptive lighting system that allows shifts in coloration through the year, as well as during the day. Brass details close the gaps in the construction and provide armrests fully integrated into the form.

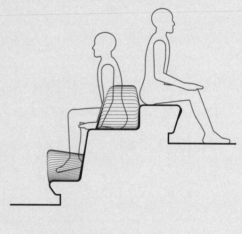

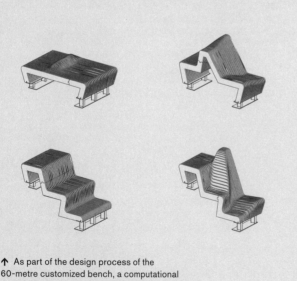

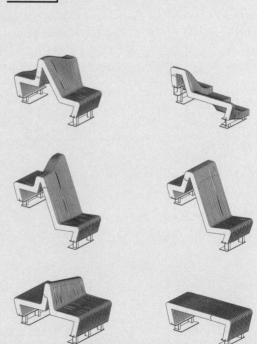

↑ As part of the design process of the 60-metre customized bench, a computational design system was developed to ensure a well-functioning, ergonomically sound and rationally manufacturable public piece of furniture.

Overleaf: The Forumtorget Bench is a 65-metre-long piece of public furniture on which everyone can find their favourite seat.

The 'seatscape' is designed to bridge the differing ground levels of the square. At night, the transparent slabs are lit from within, creating an inviting light sculpture.

Tele2 Arena

Stockholm, Sweden
Completed 2013

Nordic light, transparency and democracy were driving the design vision of Stockholm's Tele2 Arena, one of the world's most advanced international stadiums. As a hybrid between an outdoor stadium and an indoor arena, it has the flexibility to host a range of large-scale sporting and cultural events. With its overall welcoming appearance and unobstructed sightlines for spectators, the multi-purpose complex has been designed to create a memorable experience for every visitor. The arena is a crucial part of a regeneration of the Johanneshov urban district, an inviting and accessible destination with exceptional environmental credentials.

The sweeping, basket-braid perforated metal façade lends transparency and light to the arena, both inside and out. The façade allows visual experiences in both directions, revealing the excitement and laughter within, while offering panoramic views out across the city from an elevated vantage point. In fact, from the light-flooded interior communication areas, there are views of the city in all directions. The reflective façade mesh changes character according to daylight and season, and LED technology ramps behind the panels can activate any colour scheme all around the façade. The sliding roof gives the building a great deal of flexibility; for example, a football match can take place in rain while spectators sit dry in their comfortable chairs. The roof consists of eight parts, assembled in groups of four and forming two halves. Closing it takes approximately 20 minutes.

The arena has fixed seating for 30,000 people, but can accommodate another 2,000 seats for football matches, and over 40,000 guests for concerts. Inevitably, circulation was a critical design consideration, as large numbers of people need to enter and exit safely and without congestion. Generous open areas and stairwells allow people to navigate

the building with ease. Furthermore, environmentally conscious ways to get to and from the arena were promoted by improving connectivity to neighbouring areas. Visitors have the option to cycle or walk easily to the arena. Pedestrian connections to nearby subway stations were strengthened, while approximately 1,000 new bicycle parking spaces were added, contributing to Johanneshov's urban development.

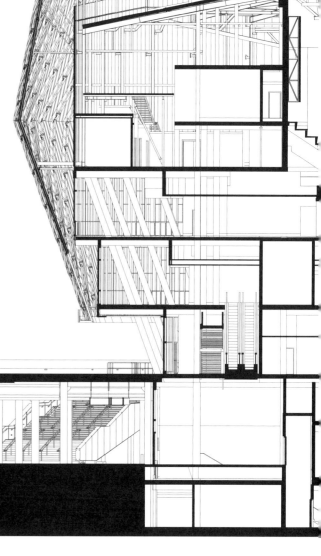

↓ Cross-section of Stockholm's Tele2 Arena, one of the world's most advanced international stadiums.

Overleaf left and right: The sliding roof functions smoothly in any weather. The limited size of the location guided the design, resulting in a building that widens towards the top.

Heden Exercise Park

Gothenburg, Sweden
Completed 2014

Where there used to be a bleak gravel car park, the people of Gothenburg can now enjoy a 24/7 outdoor gym park and field for ball games. At Heden, everybody can find an activity suitable for their age and ability, plus places to perspire, rest or stroll. Adults and children can find both workout and play areas next to one another. The gym tools are specially adapted to seniors, and what works for them works for most people. The ground is the main design feature: soft sand as flooring, gently sculpted mounds, and a wooden path for maximum accessibility. A swathe of mountain cherry trees, silver birches and pines contribute to a coherent structure that will, over time, grow to become a green roof over various portions of the park. Accessible and health-promoting public spaces are a natural part of the equitable city. Being open air, free to enter at any time and right at the heart of the city, these spaces make good sense.

→ Heden Exercise Park is a 24-hour park and outdoor gym in a site at the heart of Gothenburg that used to be a car park.

↓ & Opposite: Designed as an outdoor area for all ages, Heden is a place to exercise, play and relax.

Inspiring learning environments encourage creativity, collaboration and critical thought. Spaces are designed to adapt as pedagogical practices evolve, rethinking the traditional classroom to support different forms of learning. Places to socialize and connections to the outdoors are as important as the teaching spaces themselves, creating the best conditions for academic achievement. These buildings are also intended for wider community use, promoting social cohesion and diversity, while reinvigorating an area's economy.

In its many forms, culture is a driver for innovation and positive social transformation. The concept of culture is wide – we understand it both in terms of the ways of life in society and its system of socially transmitted patterns and narratives, and in terms of cultural activity as expressions of creativity and humanism. As architects we deal with both these understandings. Where culture thrives, society is capable of integration and social mobility; these places exhibit higher growth rates and more inclusive attitudes. Culture enriches the soul and substance of a community.

Through inspiring co-design with diverse local groups, testing new prototypes and embedding art indoors and outdoors, we can make a positive change to our communities. We extend the Right of Public Access – a tradition that provides a unique accessibility to Swedish nature – to cultural places where people come together to make and change history. Multi-purpose buildings enable new meetings and make people feel part of something bigger.

MEET, LEARN AND CREATE

Väven Cultural Centre

Umeå, Sweden
Completed 2014

The cultural centre in the northern city of Umeå is called Väven (the Weave) for several reasons. It weaves together the old and the new, interlaces various strands of urban walks and directions, undulates between city and river shore, and ties together people and culture in a great variety of activities. Väven is Sweden's second largest cultural centre, and it is housed in a new type of building that combines a diversity of disciplines within a cluster of flexible spaces.

Umeå is a busy and cultured city, a university town with a young population. The indigenous Sami culture is a part of its diversity and history. Occupying a central riverside location beside the town hall, Väven was an important landmark that spearheaded the city's creative renaissance. Designed by White in collaboration with Snøhetta, Väven is a testament to sustainable, culturally led urban regeneration. It provides hotel accommodation, conference space, meeting rooms and restaurants, a cinema, library and art gallery, plus the Women's History Museum.

The exterior is a tribute to the ubiquitous northern birch trees and their slender white trunks. In fact, Umeå is called the 'city of birch trees', many of them planted as protective barriers after the big fire of 1888, which destroyed large parts of the timber town. The white glow of *Väven* façade is achieved by a balanced mixture of laminated glass and foil, developed to reflect the Nordic light, which is limited but rich in nuance. The architecture of the cultural centre takes its cue from the mesh of activities and functions it serves by wrapping the building in one homogeneous façade. The interior space, with bare wood flooring and ribbed ceilings, provides flexible accommodation for all kinds of activity. The colour palette used in the interior recalls birch leaves through the seasons, from tender green buds to autumn golds and winter frost. Careful consideration was given to air, noise and light to create a healthy indoor environment.

Residents, local businesses and cultural departments, as well as private and municipal funding bodies, contributed to the planning process through in-depth interviews and workshops. Umeå's locals wanted a place where they could play a lively and active part in cultural life, and the architecture is created in response to a variety of activities. This is perhaps the building's true achievement: managing to incorporate a multitude of hopes and wishes into one unified structure.

↓ Elevations, clockwise from top left: west, south, north, east.

→ The white façade of Umeå's cultural centre Väven makes it a striking landmark, especially when seen against the clear Nordic sky and the waters of Umeälven river.

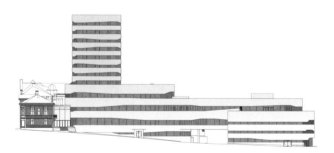

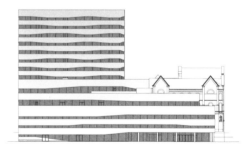

Bråtejordet Secondary School

Strømmen, Norway
Completed 2014

Strømmen, formerly an industrial town on the outskirts of Oslo, has been transformed into a residential area of the city, and the school is the first of its buildings to be completed. This seems fitting, as it allows young people to be the pioneers of the new community.

The local authority ran an open competition to decide on the design of the new school, and White was the winner. From the beginning of the design process, it was clear to us that the school needed to be a social stage as well as a dedicated workspace for students and teachers. The architecture therefore promotes concentration and peace for study in some spaces, while supporting lively social activity in others.

Set within an agricultural landscape, the building embraces a south-facing playground, which has astounding views. All the classrooms are on the cooler, quieter side of the campus to optimize the conditions for peaceful study.

The school is organized as a succession of four spatial analogies: *tunet* – the yard, *platået* – the plateau, *boksen* – the box, and *rommet* – the room. Tunet is the playground, which faces the sun and has open views. It is divided into landscaped fields for play and social interaction, with multi-game areas where students can burn off energy in the sunshine and fresh air. For those who want quieter interaction, there is also strategically placed seating shielded from the wind. *Platået* houses public functions, such as the school's reception area, which opens on to the exterior view from a modest elevation of the main floor area. The *platået* level gives direct access the design and technology workshops, music studios, the library and the administration block, all gathered around the central foyer, which also functions as an assembly hall and canteen. The second-floor *boksen* houses the middle-school year-groups and their amenities. Each box has its own staircase to the ground-floor central foyer, which streamlines circulation. *Rommet* provides quiet classrooms facing the landscape rather than the playground, thus minimizing distractions from the outside.

Designed to meet the most rigorous European energy-efficiency standards, Bråtejordet Secondary School combines traditionally defined boundaries with inspiring learning spaces to create the best environment for academic achievement.

↓ → The materials, both exterior and interior, were chosen from a 100-year perspective, their functionality and sustainability being designed to last for at least a century.

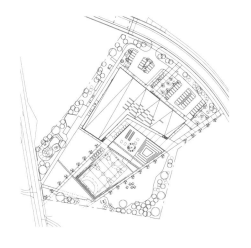

← The school's northeast façade (see also bottom drawing below).

↑ Location plan, which shows how the school sits in the landscape and is surrounded by newly planted trees.

→ The playground seating area and the building's southwest façade.

↓ Top: Elevation facing southeast, with a section showing top-floor classrooms and two double-height gymnasiums. Bottom: Elevation facing northeast.

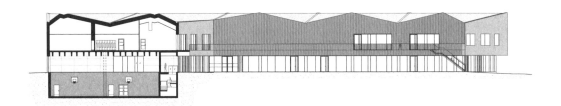

Dynamic Daylight in Schools

White Research Lab 2015

Light affects everybody – our mood, health, comfort and performance. Our light environments are a compound of daylight and artificial light, and the latter can be divided into 'temperatures': cold light and warm white light. Research studies have shown that cold light, which is at the blue end of the spectrum, has a positive effect on reading performance and the ability to concentrate, while warm white light has a positive effect on collaborative activities.

In response to research studying performance in different light conditions, a market has emerged for so-called dynamic light. This refers to light conditions that can be automatically or manually controlled to switch between cold and warm light. The receptors (rods and cones) in the human eye deal with incoming light, but there is also a third receptor, which informs our biological clock and diurnal rhythm. This inner clock is informed by light conditions and controls the body's levels of melatonin (the sleep hormone) and cortisol (the stress hormone). Cortisol production increases with higher levels of illumination and in cold white light.

One of the development networks at White is dedicated to light, a research platform that continually educates and inspires our practice. Its research report is a compilation of topical and relevant studies presented in relation to a period of intense planning of buildings for education. However, we must constantly update our knowledge and the way we live because work environments also undergo constant change. In the workplace, for example, computer screens and the light they emit are now common. It perhaps comes as no surprise that dynamic light has been successfully applied in workplaces, healthcare architecture and learning environments. As people spend more time in artificially lit spaces, architects need to develop sustainable and stimulating lighting strategies that carefully complement the use of daylight with artificial light. The stimulating character of daylight includes intensity, direction and colour.

The effect of light on focus and energy is universal, but with individual variations. Our ambition is to create architecture with optimized daylight conditions and to complement it with sustainable dynamic systems to promote the learning capacity and social atmosphere within environments where people spend a lot of time.

The large windows in this classroom optimize the amount of natural daylight it receives, but the dynamic lighting system adjusts the light levels according to the specific conditions outside and inside.

Skellefteå Cultural Centre

Skellefteå, Sweden
Competition proposal 2017

'Side by Side' is the name of White's winning entry for the competition to design a cultural centre in Skellefteå, just below the Arctic Circle in northern Sweden. The activities dancing cheek to cheek within this timber building are the Västerbotten Theatre, the Museum Anna Nordlander, the city art gallery and the public library. Hotel accommodation and meeting facilities are also available, so the building merits its welcoming central position in Skellefteå.

The cultural centre is right in the middle of Skellefteå, so it is readily available to locals and visitors alike. Its inclusion of accommodation harks back to the *kyrkby* (church village) hospitality of northern Sweden. In a thinly populated area, a trip to the nearest church could be a full day's journey, so staying overnight was common during festivities and the rituals connected to the circle of life, such as baptisms, weddings and funerals. Many churches were surrounded by a ring of lodging houses, so the implicit message was 'come for the sermon, stay for the party'. The winning proposal for the cultural centre mimics the traditional *kyrkby*, while updating the concept to a secularized society. At 18 storeys, it reflects the local tradition of tall timber architecture and, like the churches it mimics, is a beacon for community activity, though not necessarily of a religious character.

Given this historical background, and the region's forestry industry, timber informs the design proposal. The cultural centre is composed of ready-made cross-laminated timber (CLT) modules stacked between two CLT cores. A hybrid of glue-laminated timber and steel construction will allow an open-plan space that is able to accommodate all the different activities it supports. Flexibility of use permeates the plan, and includes elements such as retractable walls, which allow rooms to be expanded or subdivided according to the activity taking place within. Local and traditional timber know-how, along with recent developments in engineered timber technology, allow spectacular architectural and structural possibilities. Collaboration with the Norwegian structural engineers Florian

Kosche led to the development of two different hybrid construction systems – one for the cultural centre and another for the hotel. The structural glazing will reflect the sky and reveal the interior's exposed wood-framed signature ceiling. The centre is designed to be energy efficient and endure all weathers, so its green roof contributes to thermal insulation, functions as a noise barrier, promotes biodiversity and allows rainwater to be absorbed and/or stored for future use.

The different functions of the cultural centre will be visible from the outside, and the ground floor will be open, with entrances from several directions as a way of contributing to a dynamic city. Together with the new travel hub, the cultural centre creates new connections and paves the way for new bicycle and pedestrian routes through Skellefteå.

This 76-metre high, 19-storey structure will be Scandinavia's tallest building using a wood frame construction. More importantly, though, it will renew the idea of the *kyrkby* community, bringing people together to form collective memories inside this combined home for the arts and its visitors.

↙ Plan of first floor.

↓ 18th-floor plan (below). The top floor of the tower is a restaurant with exquisite views over Skellefteå and its surrounding landscape.

↓ 4th-floor plan (bottom) showing the Västerbottensteatern stage, the black-box stage, conference rooms, rehearsal rooms and access to terraces.

→ The glazing provides the hotel rooms with views that stretch for miles.

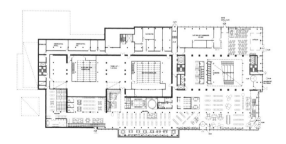

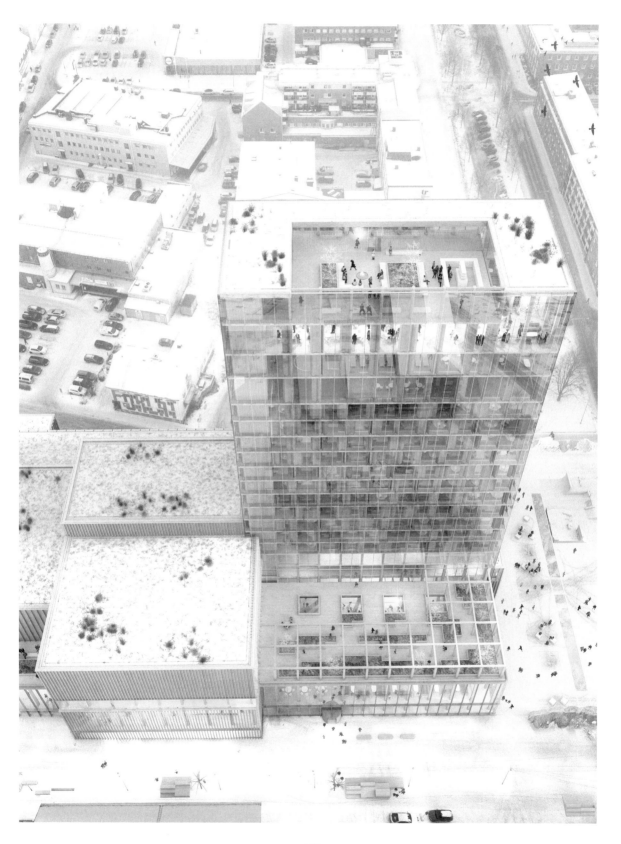

← South elevation facing the city's main square.

↑ Location plan showing how the centre fits its central location and connects to the public square by the main entrance.

→ Top-floor restaurant. In summer, the setting northern sun renders the glazed timber building in liquid gold.

↓ The lobby with its 'cultural stairs' acts as an extension of the public square.

Færder Technical College

Tønsberg, Norway
Completed 2014

Færder Technical College is a new campus for vocational learning in Tønsberg, Norway's oldest town. The campus is formed of three existing schools under one roof – a new building that provides a state-of-the-art learning environment for design, building trades, automotive mechanics and engineering. The campus is designed to be an active part of wider community life, as well as the starting point for the regeneration of Tønsberg's historic industrial seaport. The campus was the start of the economic and infrastructural regeneration of the quays, but it was also a place to revive the practical trades and skills that the area was once widely known for, such as carpentry, welding and mechanical engineering.

The client's brief was very clear: we had to convey architecturally that each and every student who set foot in this building would be a great asset to the community and society at large. Analysis of the site and principal sightlines led to the design of three key meeting places within the campus. These social spaces governed the overall form of the 15,000-square-metre building.

Færder's raw material palette consists of concrete and wood, providing excellent heat retention. They also make an exceptional contribution to the building's cooling strategies, which use water from the adjacent canal in the summer, while a highly reflective rooftop reduces initial heat build-up.

The diamond-shaped inner courtyard is designed to incorporate maximum daylight. The spatial plan is based on a vertical sequence, where the entrance hall, dining hall, auditorium and exhibition area create a large community room where the entire school can gather under one roof. Workshops and theatrical rooms on all levels are adjacent to this community room. At the heart of the building sits the 'hangar', a partially enclosed superstructure where student and public walkways converge. The hangar is a place where workshops, concerts and exhibitions can be held by both students and the public, anchoring the college within Tønsberg's community life.

↓ A semi-enclosed inner courtyard allows student and public walkways to converge.

→ Two perspectives of the central hall, which functions as a place for meeting, socializing or simply passing through.

Bildmuseet

Umeå, Sweden
Completed 2012

How can precious daylight and fragile art work in partnership? And how can the experience of moving around an exhibition space inform the architecture? These questions underpinned the design of Bildmuseet, the art museum in Umeå designed by Henning Larsen Architects and White. In this northern town, daylight is scarce, so visitors require well-lit indoor public spaces. Art, on the other hand, requires very delicately guided daylight. The interplay between natural light and the gallery lighting is dictated by the layout of windows and niches. These are orientated so that artworks get no direct exposure to daylight, but they still allow visitors to enjoy the riverside view.

Bildmuseet has seven floors devoted to art, film and a programme of international, existential, political and philosophical events, including performances and debates. The building completed Umeå's education and culture cluster along the Umeälven river, which includes the Academy of Fine Arts, the Institute of Design and the School of Architecture. The buildings are clad in

Siberian larch panels that exude a warm glow of colour, but they will eventually weather to silvery grey.

The first part of the creative campus was the School of Architecture, inaugurated in 2010. Bildmuseet is interlinked with the Institute of Design and the Academy of Fine Arts, forming a creative environment for education and research in architecture, design, art and digital culture. The synergy between the institutions is physically manifested by the architectural link, and in effect manifested in continuous cross-fertilizing connections.

↓ The main entrance to the museum is on the southeast side of Bildmuseet, which fronts the promenade along the river.

→ Bildmuseet is connected to its neighbouring building, the Institute of Design and the Academy of Fine Arts, via a shared entrance hall on the ground floor.

↑ Carefully positioned windows combine with exhibition lighting to ensure that artwork gets enough light to aid viewing, but not so much as to cause damage.

↓ The entrance and reception floor contains shops and a multi-purpose conference hall. The reception desk repeats the wood panelling of the exterior.

↑ The sculptural south stairwell offers a new vista for each floor.

→ With large windows towards the Umeälven river, the interior is flooded with daylight.

Selma Community Centre

Gothenburg, Sweden
Concept design 2017

The activity is the ornament in Selma Community Centre. The façade will become a stage, showcasing the many activities inside, seen through the softly draped openings. The building houses the Norra Hisingen town hall, plus an array of public activities, including a library, theatre, café and restaurant, multi-purpose spaces, meeting and media rooms, and halls for music and dance.

Combining culture and local administration, this multi-purpose town hall is at the centre of a regenerated city region that is growing around Selma Lagerlöfs Square. The square is named after a well-known Swedish author, the first woman to receive the Nobel Prize in Literature. Although the square is a visual extension of the community centre, the building does not turn its back to either side of its location. All four façades are constructed with the same consideration to detail in raw corrugated concrete with stretches of warm, copper-toned metal. There is equal visual and physical communication between exterior and interior on all four sides of the building. The Hisings Backa region of Gothenburg was developed during the years of the Million Homes Programme, the ambitious public housing project that Sweden achieved between 1965 and 1974. In the rejuvenation programme of Hisings Backa, culture and social activities are guiding the process to form a strong local community with great opportunities for self-expression.

↓ An exploded view of the community centre, showing the range of activities it supports, and the principal daylight scheme.

→ The graceful curves above the windows resemble stage curtains, framing the activities inside.

↘ The activities of the interior, such as dance, become performative ornaments of the façade.

The GoDown Arts Centre in Nairobi:
Building for a young democracy

ARQ Research Project 2015

When the GoDown Arts Centre opened in 2003, it was the first truly local centre for contemporary arts and innovative culture in Kenya. Inspired by the need for just such a meeting point, its conceptualization carried the aspirations of the emergent culture sector. Today, in the same inventive spirit and with a firm understanding of the unifying power of culture, the centre is laying the foundations for a democratic future and generating inspiration around a model of community-healing architecture.

When Kenya achieved independence from Britain in 1963, the country had to face a number of problems. More than 42 different ethnic groups, who had been deliberately pitted against one another during the colonial era, suddenly had to work together to establish (among other things) land ownership arrangements. Inevitably, tension flared up from time to time, particularly during elections, and 2007 stands out as perhaps one of the lowest points. Fortunately, a belief in the principles of democracy served to restore stability and informed the brokering of a living arrangement. The GoDown played its part by mounting the 'Kenya Burning' exhibition, forcing a reckoning with the horror of civil strife.

From its inception, the GoDown has grown in response to the need for Kenyan and East African artists to come together in a mutually supportive space. It is situated in an old warehouse in the industrial area, south of the railway. The current transformation of this area offers new opportunities, signalling great possibilities for the entire GoDown block to be an accessible public space. The GoDown has a dual aim: to provide an improved home for artists and creative industries, while offering valuable public services that anchor the building in community life. It is designed not only to add vitality to the street life, but also to ensure, through its community-building activities, that it is an actively democratic space.

The research conducted in relation to this project was done through workshops and online initiatives, generating ideas and proposals directly based on the robust agenda of the GoDown community. This included artists and creative entrepreneurs, as well as schoolchildren, local businesses, city representatives and the general public. The process is an ongoing dialogue, so the ensuing designs are continually energized, refreshed and reflected upon.

GoDown hosts a variety of events, all with a spirit of community that with time will claim the former industrial area of Nairobi as a cultural meeting point.

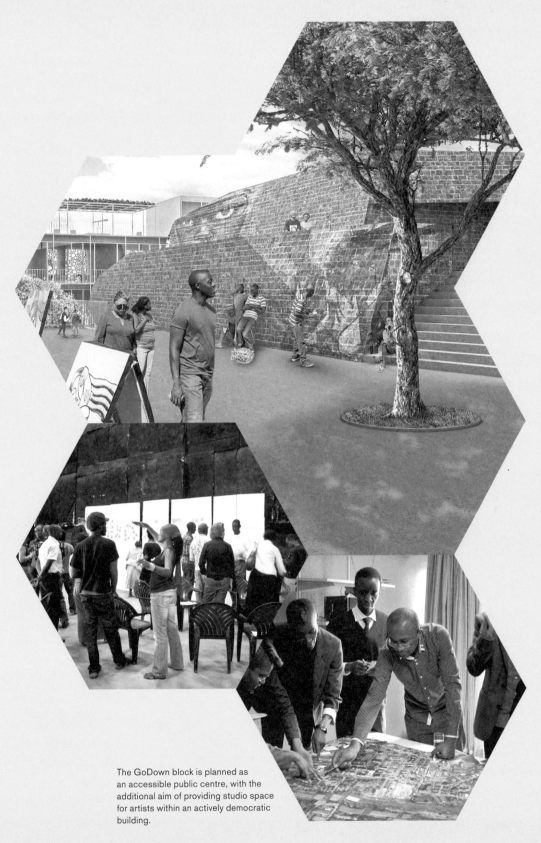

The GoDown block is planned as an accessible public centre, with the additional aim of providing studio space for artists within an actively democratic building.

The researchers and architects organizing the series of conversations between multi-stakeholders and the GoDown gathered the outcomes into a focused structural plan for the railway area to the north of GoDown, integrating sustainability into all aspects of it. This was submitted to Nairobi City Council as the revised Nairobi Master Plan (NIUPLAN 2014/2015), the first since 1973, and a good relationship developed. White and the GoDown then presented part of this work together in 2014 at the World Urban Forum in Medellín, Colombia. It was called 'Urban Equity in Development – Cities for Life'.

For more than a decade, the GoDown has served as a home, workplace, meeting point and address for artists, and has contributed to their stability, legitimacy, visibility and creative confidence. The strength of the GoDown, as Kenya's leading platform for cultural exchange, lies in the programming diversity. Core activities of music, dance and the arts run alongside major international conferences, such as the East Africa Arts Summit, but also encompass local events and gatherings such as the Dunda Mtaani youth festival. In addition, education is supported through courses such as the Creative Entrepreneurship Program and the Harvard Copyright Course. The GoDown is a place for everyone.

Through its exhibitions, the GoDown has contributed to a deeper understanding of the need for cultural infrastructure as a democratic common ground in Nairobi. The key achievement has been the establishment of relations between previously antagonistic communities. Under the title 'Never Forget, Never Again', a photographic exhibition was launched at the centre in April 2008 and has since toured the country before every election. The GoDown's close relationship with the creative community has also resulted in the urban annual festival *Nai Ni Who?* (Who Is Nairobi?). This enquiry was a way of exploring and developing urban identity in collaboration with the citizens of Nairobi. Powered by the success of

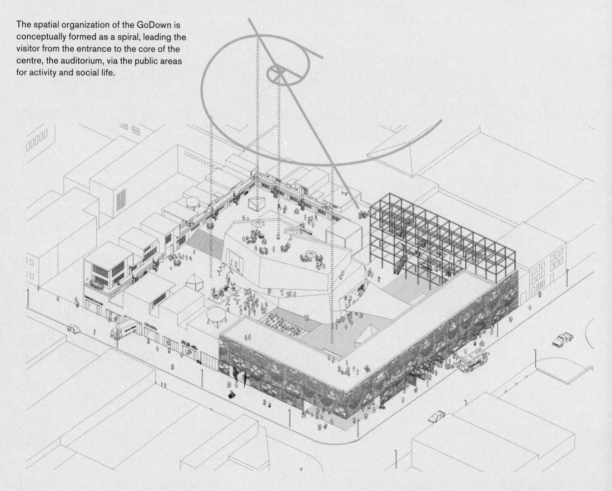

The spatial organization of the GoDown is conceptually formed as a spiral, leading the visitor from the entrance to the core of the centre, the auditorium, via the public areas for activity and social life.

its programming, the GoDown is aiming to step up its capacity and expand its role as a free space for Kenyans, while opening up to the international scene.

During White Arkitekter's study trip to Nairobi in 2010, a constructive and friendly relationship was established with the GoDown thanks to a mutual interest in architecture as a community-empowering process. White was subsequently engaged to find supportive tools and methods for a complex multi-stakeholder process. A number of workshops and seminars followed, including analyses of the streetscape. Dialogues were aimed at formulating ways of creating a vibrant, sustainable environment integrating various existing players and collecting information that all parties involved could share and build upon. Swedish partners included the cultural sector developer Mimeta, Kulturhuset Stockholm and the Museum of Architecture. One of the most important questions raised was: 'How can a new cultural space be financed in an economy lacking public funds?' Joy

Mboya, executive director of the GoDown, provided the answer: 'The money is in the vision.' In other words, the architectural process would be a way of getting people to 'buy into' the project. Gathering around a visionary process would bring more people to the table where the exchange of ideas was taking place. The role of the architects has been to accommodate the ideas and visualize the dialogue into a model proposal, which in turn generates interest and financial support from the community. The vision is both a financial and democratizing cornerstone of the future building.

As architects, we have been able to take a guiding role in the process of finding a common vision and directing the energy of the discussions towards a design solution. Fundraising has begun and is hoped to be achieved by 2020.

Nai Ni Who? (Who Is Nairobi?) is an annual festival initiated by the GoDown to explore and develop urban identity with the inhabitants of the city.

The GoDown Arts Centre

Nairobi, Kenya
Concept design 2014

The new GoDown Arts Centre is organized around three courtyards on three different levels. The largest, on the ground floor, is designed as an impressive welcoming space, with a large tree adding shade and character. This main courtyard can accommodate hundreds of visitors, and includes in the northern part an area for children, art activities and play. This area also connects an exhibition space, library, auditorium, museum, atelier, offices and a restaurant. The auditorium itself is an interesting architectural object within the main courtyard, complete with a rooftop restaurant. A wide staircase leads up to a second courtyard, where there are spaces for creative studios and dance. In the third and most intimate courtyard are visual artist studios, arranged in duplex formations. Underground car parking frees up the courtyards for leisure activities, such as open-air performances and skating. Additional film and music studios are also in the basement. The New GoDown will have 12,000 square metres of indoor space and 10,000 square metres outdoors.

As a node in the current transformation of Nairobi's industrial area, the cultural centre fills a need for public space in the urban development process. One of its key achievements has been to establish meaningful relations between diverse Nairobi communities through conversations, as well as through singular and cross-cultural activities. The push for self-understanding along with a wider cohesiveness means that self-awareness is growing, and resulting in integrated neighbourhoods that enhance Kenyan artistic and cultural life.

The main façade of GoDown, as well as the spatial organization around the courtyards, is inspired by fractals. These mathematical patterns are the building blocks of the natural world and recur in man-made environments. From the arrangement of villages to hair-braiding patterns, fractals are omnipresent in Kenyan culture, and in Africa as a whole. The permeability of the façade helps to convey the idea of openness, even though the entire centre can be locked down after hours. Façade detailing options are currently being investigated in collaboration with local architects at Planning Systems and artists connected with the centre.

The GoDown aims to manage diversity in many ways, not least by supporting well-being, creativity and human exchange. The development of both the centre and the site will act as a catalyst for the regeneration of the entire area and serve to connect different parts of the city. White is proud to contribute to the next chapter of the GoDown story: a vibrant cultural space and 'living room' for all Nairobians, Kenyans and their guests. This story will express the freedom and fellowship that starts with a bigger Kenyan 'we'.

↓ The façade of the GoDown, to be designed in collaboration with local artists, will convey identity, while also incorporating climate conditioning layers.

↑ This visualization is merely an impression of what the façade pattern might be.

Messingen

Upplands Väsby, Sweden
Completed 2011

The range of activities in the multi-use complex Messingen is the result of careful research involving all users of the building, who are united in their support of it being the heart of the community. The building sits at the centre of the Upplands Väsby region, north of Stockholm and next to the busy railway station. The multi-purpose sports, cultural and conference facilities it contains, along with a café, restaurant and waiting room for the adjacent station, mean that the building buzzes with life from early in the morning until late at night.

The story behind the complex began with the local council commissioning White to design a new high school in a run-down area. After analysing the situation and realizing that there was a need for a public multi-purpose hub as well as a school, a completely new plan emerged. The co-location of the two buildings has been very successful because the students have benefited from the readily accessible sports activities, cultural events and library, as well as good transport links provided by the station. Visitors to conferences and events happily mix with the students, who in turn are proud and helpful hosts. Those looking for a quieter meeting place can use the café, and members of the public can take up study opportunities offered by the centre. Visitors and students alike access the complex through a shared entrance. Indeed, the mixing of generations is one of the building's greatest assets, empowering the young, who naturally

act as guiding residents to the more temporary visitors. Since its opening in 2011, the new Väsby Senior High School in Messingen has begun attracting pupils from other municipalities, and more enterprises are moving into the building.

The façade of the complex is industrial in character, reminiscent of the site's history. Externally, the design comprises perforated sheet metal of varying transparency, which 'dissolves' the simple cubic shape. Corten steel ribs constitute external sun screening, providing colour and a contrast to the glazed sections of the building. The roof is planted with sedum, which captures acidic rain that would otherwise end up in the surface water drains. Sedum roofs also maintain a more even temperature inside the building, while simultaneously absorbing air pollution, reducing noise and absorbing surface water. The building volume is compact and therefore energy efficient, minimizing the amount of material used in the façades.

↓ → The sleek lines of the Messingen complex inspire pride in its students, while the range of activities and facilities available to the public make it a popular local hub.

↓ Open teaching environments complement ordinary classrooms and provide spaces for new working methods.

→ Visitors to conferences and events overlap with students in the shared parts of the complex. This creates a good relationship between the generations.

The Humanities Theatre

Uppsala, Sweden
Completed 2017

Uppsala University English Park Campus is home to the departments of humanities, theology and social sciences. The Humanities Theatre is the newest addition to the campus – a theatre designed to stimulate open and democratic dialogue for faculty and public alike. Its 140 seats are placed in a horseshoe arrangement on a steep gradient around a central area. This layout enables all present to make eye contact with one another. It is not a space for passive audiences, but a place where everyone can participate within the intimate grandeur of an amphitheatre setting. A strong inspiration for this project has been the Gustavianum Anatomical Theatre, a unique piece of academic architecture on the university campus, constructed by Olof Rudbeck in 1662.

The new auditorium's design allows voices to be heard from any seat, thanks to the integrated system of microphones and speakers placed in the ceiling above both audience and stage. The acoustics can also be adjusted to create the ambience required, for example, the sound of a church or even a cave.

The Humanities Theatre is a new public forum that encourages cross-disciplinary dialogue among faculties, as well as between the university and community, on a local, national and international scale. This is facilitated by an interactive display measuring 32 square metres, which opens the debate to those participating through digital channels.

The curved exterior is clad with bronze-coloured aluminium sheets perforated with hexagonal patterns. This façade is a piece of public art, designed by the artist Ann Lislegaard. Treated as a separate commission for the Public Art Agency Sweden, the artist's concept was translated into the architecture by the development network Dsearch.

↓ → The perforated façade of the theatre beautifully complements the design. At night, the backlit panels add a sense of depth to the building.

Overleaf, left: The theatre springs surprises from every direction.

Overleaf, right: The striking red interior of the auditorium contrasts with the colours elsewhere in the theatre.

Billingskolan

Skövde, Sweden
Completed 2014

'*Oculus*', the Latin word for 'eye', was the name of this winning proposal for a school of 350 children aged between 6 and 12. As an architectural term, oculus describes high-set windows and top lights, famously featured in Rome's Pantheon. Why not include this element in a school in Skövde?

The architectural agenda for Billingskolan focuses on the way children perceive their environment. Oculus is a solitary building, with all its facilities, including the sports hall, under the same roof. The principal structure of top-lit boxes grouped around a central indoor hub provides great flexibility of use and also the possibility of future additions.

Billingskolan has five distinct spaces, each with their own 'periscope' light well. The five parts are grouped around a central hall space, where an open-air atrium draws light into the heart of the school. The periscopes rise from the school's roofline and channel daylight into the colourful interior. These semi-glazed units are more like studios than traditional classrooms, serving to maximize daylight and promote well-being. The location of windows was carefully planned to achieve optimal climate and lighting conditions. This, along with considerations about mass, orientation and materials, supported the sustainability strategy that led to the Gold level awarded by the Sweden Green Building Council, making Billingskolan one of the most environmentally sustainable schools in Sweden.

↓ Colourful skylights from periscope-like towers draw light into the school during the day. At night, these are lit artificially.

→ The striking open-air atrium is a light-well around which the canteen is situated.

↘ The south-facing playground offers lots of sporting activities.

The Street of Lights

White Research Lab 2016

A thousand lanterns, crafted by a thousand children, light up the darkest winter night in Bergsjön. The alley is filled with light and people, songs and speeches, celebrating the joint effort put into the occasion. The 400-metre string of lights resulted from one of White's Light Lab workshops for children, where the creative learning process is just as important as finding your own lantern suspended among 999 others. Getting children and young people directly involved in a positive transformation of the public environment was an ambition of this research-based collaboration project.

The Street of Lights was created by children aged 6–9, who were invited to explore the phenomenon of light in 100 workshops. Among the participants was the local primary school, where refugee children and recently arrived families make their first connections and start settling into the community. The installation physically connected the property owners on both sides of the street, but, more importantly, it brought together in one place newly arrived citizens, children of all ages, the civic authorities and commercial actors – a clear demonstration of democracy at work in and for public space.

The project is a collaboration between White, GöteborgsOperan and the Swedish Exhibition Agency, and many driving forces in and around Bergsjön, including the local council in eastern Gothenburg, the City of Gothenburg's Cultural Affairs Administration, Konstepidemin Arts and Cultural Centre, and the University of Gothenburg. More than 100 local associations were invited to the Street of Lights, and the project was widely reported in social media and the press. In almost all cultures, light is synonymous with hope. The installation might be temporal, but hope is eternal.

From the workshops that created it to the interested parties who installed it, the Street of Lights has brought the community of Bergsjön together.

The Public Light Lab

White Research Lab 2016

Children are very receptive to the magic of light. It unites art, science and myth, it brings colours to life, and it differentiates textures and shapes. It can be shared by many, bringing a sense of security and energy, and stimulating imagination and intellect.

The Public Light Lab is an innovative social design project taking place in and around the suburban area of Bergsjön in eastern Gothenburg. This is an area with a large and growing international community, and an important multicultural heritage. During 2016 and 2017, light became the focus of aesthetic and creative design projects, with enthusiastic input from the public.

The co-production of light installations in public spaces engaged children, whose creativity had a direct impact in the local community. Light as a cultural phenomenon is a positive force, and therefore a socially unifying art form that makes a great difference in physical spaces. In collaboration with GöteborgsOperan and the Swedish Exhibition Agency, White constructed a mobile learning lab on the central square, Rymdtorget.

The programme inside this glowing pavilion reached 1,000 school children over a period of five weeks, during which 100 workshops took place. Children aged 6–9, together with their teachers, participated in an interactive expedition in this learning space.

A guide called 'Light Guardian' introduced the physical and artistic aspects of light to the children by inviting them on a metaphorical exploratory journey. Together they travelled to the moon and the sun, encountering a rainbow and discovering its spectrum of colours, then exploring shadows in the search for a character called 'Little Light'. This playful method of discovery is unifying because it does not depend on language skills. Every child brought back to their families an invitation to 'open house at the lab', where they themselves would act as guides. The open house events were very popular and attracted many people who would not otherwise have met.

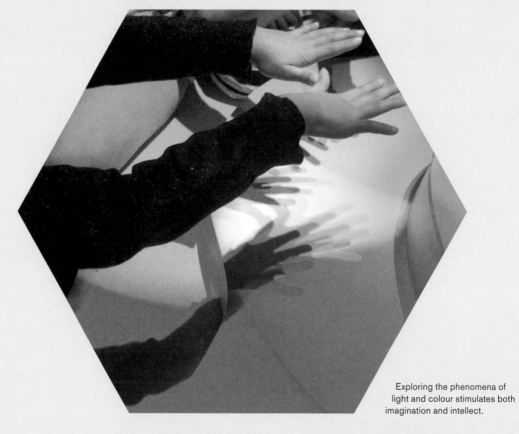

Exploring the phenomena of light and colour stimulates both imagination and intellect.

The Light Guardian takes the children on
an educational journey through different
aspects of light and space.

Cirkus Skandiascenen

Stockholm, Sweden
Completed 2015

Carved into the rock, Skandiascenen is an artfully inserted addition to the historic Cirkus Theatre at the Royal Djurgården in Stockholm. When Cirkus opened in 1892, the theatre seated 1,600 people and was home to the great Swedish circus companies of the day. Over the years it has transformed into mainly a music theatre and concert venue. With the addition of Skandiascenen, which seats 800 theatregoers, and an expanded entrance hall, the venue hosts two distinct audiences and gives improved accessibility to both.

In order to fit the extension on the small site, a large portion of Skandiascenen was carved into the underlying rock and placed below ground. The new foyer was split over two levels, linking Skandiascenen to the Cirkus Theatre and increasing the capacity for visitors when shows are held in both halls. After dark, the older building's interior façade reveals itself behind the glass volume of the lobby.

Adding new functionality to the old landmark made sense. We carefully maximized the available space by creating an extension with its own identity while showing an appreciation of Cirkus's cultural legacy.

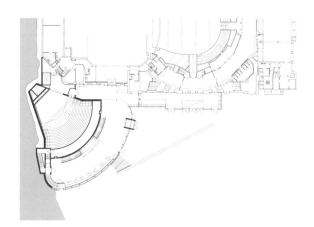

↑ Skandiascenen's stage is fitted into a seemingly impossible site, carved into the rockbed at one end and connecting to the *fin de siècle* building via the entrance hall.

↓ The addition is respectful of the site and the original Cirkus building, adding a discreet but festive elegance.

→ The new glazed foyer features a generous bar for visitors, leading downstairs to the cloakrooms and entrance.

The Right of Public Access provides a unique accessibility to Swedish nature. Some might say that, for many Swedes, dwelling in nature is a form of religion. We turn to the forests and meadows for comfort and solace, and we trust nature to replenish our energy levels. Adding buildings to our precious natural environment requires the utmost respect and attentiveness, but also confidence in designing spaces that celebrate the natural environment and benefit all living beings.

Access to public space is a foundation of democracy, and landscape architecture is a powerful tool that can help achieve this. Good landscape design strengthens our connection to nature to create uplifting outdoor spaces that enhance health and well-being. It actively boosts biodiversity, while providing resilience to climate change through strategies for better resource management. These principles – from participatory urban gardening initiatives to parkland planning – guide our design.

The world is facing the huge challenges of climate change and diminishing resources. Driving change is a responsibility that we take seriously. We aim to create zero-carbon buildings, advance timber construction and use digital tools that enhance sustainable design. By rethinking resource efficiencies, using materials with a low environmental impact and taking advantage of natural ecosystems, we design buildings and public spaces that ensure comfort and promote well-being for people, while strengthening the living world around us.

LET
NATURE
LEAD

Naturum Kosterhavet

Koster, Sweden
Completed 2012

Kosterhavet National Park was Sweden's first marine reserve, emphasizing the unique character of the Koster archipelago. Naturum Kosterhavet is a visitor centre in Ekenäs, Koster – Sweden's most westerly outpost – where sea, wind and the existing buildings of the fishing village set the tone for the project. The Swedish Environmental Protection Agency has established an outstanding architectural standard for its visitor centres – Naturum – in national parks, nature reserves, unusual habitats and world heritage sites in 33 locations around Sweden. Over the years, White has so far won nine of the Naturum design competitions, each one with a cautious footprint in relation to the unique, protected environment.

In order to meet the highest standards for energy efficiency and low carbon footprint, the building is constructed mainly from forestry-certified wood and powered by renewable energy, with a water supply from a nearby osmosis unit. Its ventilation is climate-responsive, and geothermal heating is employed throughout. Each Naturum is an exemplar of innovative climate-responsible solutions thanks to the ambitious level of sustainable performance that keeps pushing the standard for every centre that is built.

Naturum Kosterhavet stands by the water's edge on filled and reclaimed ground. Timber panels clad its roof and façades, reflecting the coastal building tradition of the nearby fishing village of Ekenäs. The pleated roof forms a wave, and its intricate geometry is seen from the exhibition hall below, where the ceiling is part of the visitors' experience as they learn about life below the surface of the sea. The centre houses exhibition areas that tell the story of the national park, and also has an interactive aquarium, a water laboratory, lecture theatres and a library.

Many skills have been brought together to create Naturum Kosterhavet, which is as much a civic focal point as a tourist attraction. In fact, the local population, as well as politicians, were keen contributors to the project. It was essential that any change to the unique environment of this small coastal village should be made collaboratively in order to maintain the delicate balance between man and nature, something that the local community had experienced and absorbed over many generations. By being engaged at various stages of the project, which incorporated convincing design and resilience in performance, they can act as proud hosts in a welcoming building.

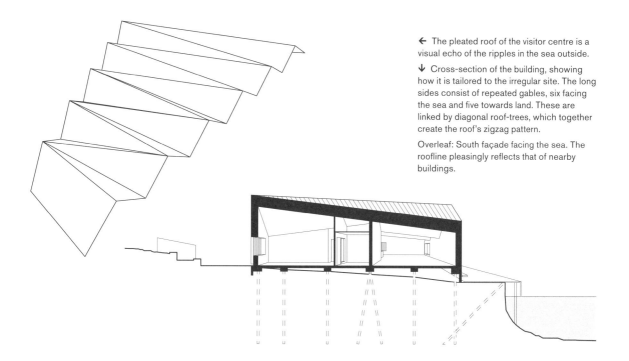

← The pleated roof of the visitor centre is a visual echo of the ripples in the sea outside.

↓ Cross-section of the building, showing how it is tailored to the irregular site. The long sides consist of repeated gables, six facing the sea and five towards land. These are linked by diagonal roof-trees, which together create the roof's zigzag pattern.

Overleaf: South façade facing the sea. The roofline pleasingly reflects that of nearby buildings.

← Aerial view of the traditional fishing village of Ekenäs in Koster and the carefully placed Naturum. The building's red timber cladding allows it to blend with the local architecture.

↓ The visitor centre is light and airy, and the view across the harbour almost appears to be one of the exhibits.

Hasle Harbour Baths

Bornholm, Denmark
Completed 2013

The small town of Hasle on the Danish island of Bornholm is renowned for its lingering sunsets. Hasle is historically important as a fishing and ferry port, but the declining fishing industry and rerouted transport lines have taken a toll on the island's economy. In an attempt to boost the tourist industry, the island commissioned White to design Hasle Harbour Baths, with the idea of making them a social gathering point where people of all ages and abilities could bathe, relax and enjoy the spectacular sea views. It consists of a floating platform with a seating landscape around a 15-metre swimming pool and a small children's pool. A corner of the platform rises to a peak, an area where people can sunbathe and which is also the locals' favourite place for a sunset picnic.

While the harbour's granite breakwaters provide safe berthing for fishing vessels, they also obstruct views out to sea. Reinstating the sea views was therefore a priority in the design of Hasle Harbour Baths. The intention was for people to walk, sit and lie on the structure, which gave rise to the design concept of an outdoor 'carpeting' that folded over the breakwaters.

Hasle Harbour Baths are connected to the shore by a 25-metre floating promenade that leads to a sauna, toilet facilities and an outdoor changing area. To the south of this is a jetty catering for a variety of water sports. The wooden stairs, promenade and outdoor furniture are composed of FSC-certified Azobe timber, selected for its aesthetic qualities as well as its ability to withstand the harsh marine environment.

↓ The children's and adults' pools sit next to each other on the floating platform.

→ ↘ The stepped seating is orientated for sunbathing as well as for enjoying the sunset. The corner peak extends over the water and incorporates diving boards.

Overleaf: The timber and concrete will tune together to form a soft grey hue over time.

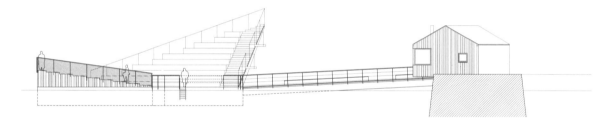

Birdwatchers' Sheaf Shack

Toronto, Canada
Competition proposal 2016

Winter Stations is an international design competition initiated to bring temporary public art installations to Toronto's winter waterfront landscape. The design proposals, intended to celebrate the area, incorporate and transform the lifeguard stations on the city's eastern beaches for the duration of the winter season.

For the third year of the competition, in 2016, our design was a biodegradable birdwatching platform. This made sense because beaches are rich habitats for many birds, and birdwatching is a great way to connect with the natural environment. It transcends age and socio-economic barriers, so it has the potential to bring people together.

White designed its entry with the help of its Dsearch development network. The Sheaf Shack is 4 metres high, with a viewing platform reached by climbing the steps of the existing lifeguard station. It is constructed like a shelving system, in which horizontal sheaves of straw and grain are stacked on top of one another in a triangular formation. The interior is cut to shape, but the exterior is left uncut so that the sheaves can be clearly seen and also provide a feeding station for birds. The appearance of the structure will therefore change over the winter, depending on the birds' feeding patterns.

Underneath the birdwatching platform, well protected from the winter winds, is a hide containing a miniature ornithology library and binoculars. The design of this structure will therefore allow people to experience wildlife very close at hand.

↓ Step-by-step plans showing timber poles with a support structure of triangular wooden shelves that keep the sheaves secure and sturdy by 'squeezing' them into place.

↗ The structure makes a twist around three vertical wooden poles to achieve its final shape.

↘ Birdwatchers can reach the roof of the platform via the steps of the existing lifeguard station within. This gives them great views of the birds coming to feed off the platform.

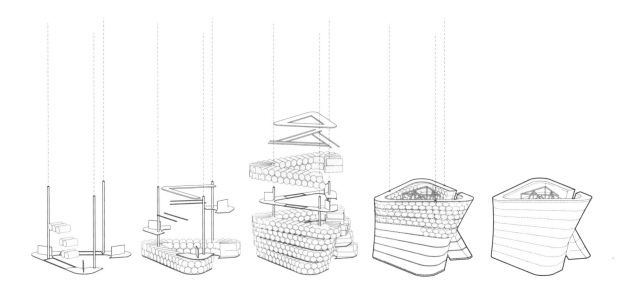

Naturum Store Mosse

Hillerstorp, Sweden
Completed 2003

Floating over the grass tussocks at the edge of the forest, Store Mosse (literally 'big bog') visitor centre overlooks the wildlife and shifting light of the landscape, while the exhibition within reveals the mysteries of this old and spongy habitat. It transports guests into the heart of folklore while recounting the region's 14,000-year history, from the Ice Age to the present day.

Floating about a metre above the unspoilt terrain, the timber building is supported by two 36-metre structural beams resting on four granite supports. This Naturum is built entirely of timber, which is crudely worked but joined with great precision. Inside, the timber is left untreated; outside, the decking and timber panelling have been protected against rot with dark brown wood tar.

The timber frame of the structure is visible from both outside and inside the building, and the exposed roof trusses, cross-braces and hangers give it an identity that complements its woodland surroundings. This Naturum is a wonderful place from which to observe the wealth of plants and wildlife around it – the sedge and willow, the swans and swifts, the dragonflies and bog myrtle.

↑ The south-facing wall, with its spaced timbers, allows the shifting light to pass through it in various patterns.

↙ Seating on the south side allows visitors to sit in comfort while viewing the surroundings.

↓ The exhibition room has a glazed short-side wall offering views over the bogland.

Naturum Vänerskärgården Victoria House

Lidköping, Sweden
Completed 2012

Naturum Vänerskärgården Victoria House is a visitor centre in the archipelago shared with the baroque Läckö Castle. The centre was built and is operated with minimal impact on its surroundings. The vertical ribs of the timber façade echo the surrounding trees and reeds, while the flowing contours of the building hint at the sweeping movement and dramatic contrasts of light and shade that characterize the baroque style of the nearby castle.

The brief for the visitor centre was to provide exhibition spaces to showcase the history of Djurö National Park and accommodate a rolling programme of events and activities, while also including a new restaurant and a 15-room hotel. The main exhibition space is furnished with a large open fire for chillier days. A generous timber deck surrounds the building, creating an additional space for play or reflection, and strengthening the connection between indoors and outdoors.

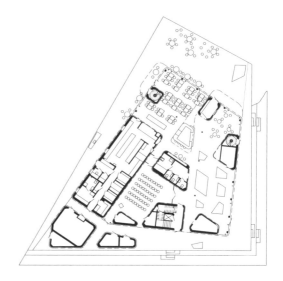

↑ A wrap-around boardwalk surrounds the ground floor of the building. On the upper floor are 15 hotel rooms with en-suite bathrooms.

↓ Nearby Läckö Castle attracts a large number of visitors every year. The Naturum was built to remind people of the riches of Europe's largest freshwater archipelago.

↑ The vertical ribs on the timber façade reflect the lakeside vegetation of trees and reeds, while varying the amount of light and shade that enters the building.

↑ The reception desk follows the triangular atrium contour, and continues the external theme of wooden uprights as decoration.

↓ Two façades on the eastern side of the building face the lovely Vänern seafront.

Free-form Timber:
From design to fabrication

Innochain and Dsearch/White Research Lab 2015

Here we showcase a PhD project, *Integrating Material Performance* by Tom Svilans, which re-examines timber in the light of developments in material sciences, digital design tools and fabrication techniques, with the aim of devising materials-driven design solutions and new structural morphologies. The result is a celebration of the architectural possibilities of glue-laminated timber.

The project is part of an EU-funded research training network called InnoChain, which brings together 15 PhD candidates, six academic institutions and 14 industry partners, including White. The network was initiated by the Centre for IT and Architecture (CITA) at the Royal Danish Academy of Fine Arts, Schools of Architecture, Design and Conservation in Copenhagen as part of the InnoChain Early Training Network, with funding from the EU's Horizon 2020 research and innovation programme. The research is affiliated with White's development network Dsearch, a design and research unit that looks at how computation can impact, support and change the way architectural projects are designed and delivered.

The project addresses three distinct but overlapping themes: the production and communication of knowledge across design, development and fabrication networks; the integration of the material performance of engineered timber into these networks through computational tools; and the application of digital sensing and acquisition tools to industrial timber fabrication workflows. The project unfolds primarily through a research-by-design method based on experiments in the form of speculative probes, prototypes and demonstrators. The method of enquiry is therefore parallel strands of physical prototyping and information modelling, drawing on the expertise of the industrial partners and the testing of workflows through workshops, case studies and architectural proposals.

One of the main objectives of this project was to connect design practice and industrial fabrication with the objective of introducing new ways of working with the material performance of laminated timber. The project was thus carried out as a collaboration between White, representing design practice, and Blumer-Lehmann, the Swiss producer of advanced timber building components, representing industrial fabrication. The role of these partners in the project is to contextualize the research through application to real-life projects and integration into wider processes of design, logistics and management.

In a further collaboration, a larger design prototype was developed to test the emerging tools and workflows in both projects. That collaboration led to our submitting a design in the folly competition at the 2017 Tallinn Architectural Biennale. It was short-listed from over 200 international entries, and won second prize in the final evaluation.

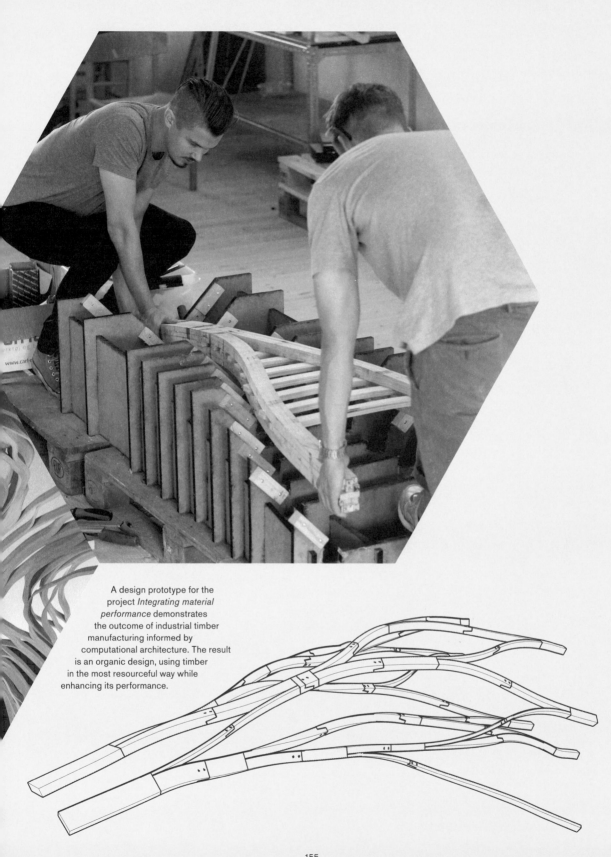

A design prototype for the project *Integrating material performance* demonstrates the outcome of industrial timber manufacturing informed by computational architecture. The result is an organic design, using timber in the most resourceful way while enhancing its performance.

The Royal Pavilion, Southend Pier

Southend-on-Sea, United Kingdom
Completed 2012

The longest British seaside pier is at Southend in Essex, and stretches 2,150 metres into the North Sea. Since its opening in 1835, this typical Victorian pleasure pier on a wrought-iron fundament has prevailed through fires, ship collisions, storms and two world wars. However, the pier gradually fell into decline, and was bought in 2009 by the borough council. In our proposal to the international design competition to breathe new life into the pier and its surroundings, we transformed it into a cultural and visitor centre constructed with recycled timber from the pier floor.

White, in collaboration with the British architectural practice Sprunt, submitted a competition entry called *Sculpted by Wind and Wave* which proposed turning the pier into a vivid urban thoroughfare. Starting as an extension of the high street, this public promenade culminates at the pier head with the Royal Pavilion. The entire structure uses materials tried and tested in boat construction: timber and wood panelling, fibreglass and aluminium. The entire pavilion was constructed on a nearby wharf and lifted on to the pier.

The Royal Pavilion includes studio spaces for artists, a restaurant and a 500-seat open-air theatre. It also hosts a year-round schedule of exhibitions, film screenings, live performances and other events. All these elements offer dramatic views of the sea and the Essex coastline.

← The location plan shows the end of the seaside pier, which extends more than 2 kilometres out to sea. The end of a small railway is visible on the far left of the plan.

↓ → The pavilion is a multifunctional space, hosting, among other events, concerts, exhibitions, conferences and weddings.

← An accessibility ramp is built into the front stairs, as a continuation of the timber boardwalk leading into the pavilion.

↓ The pavilion engages in a visually dynamic interplay with the sky, the horizon and the sea.

Karlshamn Bath House

Karlshamn, Sweden
Completed 2015

There is a long tradition of swimming in the sea in the town of Karlshamn. Now, thanks to the local community, some willing sponsors and a welcoming town council, people are able to enjoy bathing in both water and light. What drives the design of this pier is a sense of seeing and moving towards the seascape, from the narrow bridge to the warm embrace of the water. The wooden walls and sun-deck are smooth to the skin and the eye. The bath house turns away from the shoreline and opens up towards the surrounding archipelago. Inside, a shared lounge under a terraced roof is a symmetrical dividing line between the men's and women's changing rooms.

The distinctively geometric external surfaces of the pier are clad in timber panels, which have been treated with a grey-pigmented oil to protect the wood and gradually reveal its natural grain. The dark hue of the exterior matches the rocks that line the shore, while inside, untreated wood is used throughout to lend warmth and tactility for the guests.

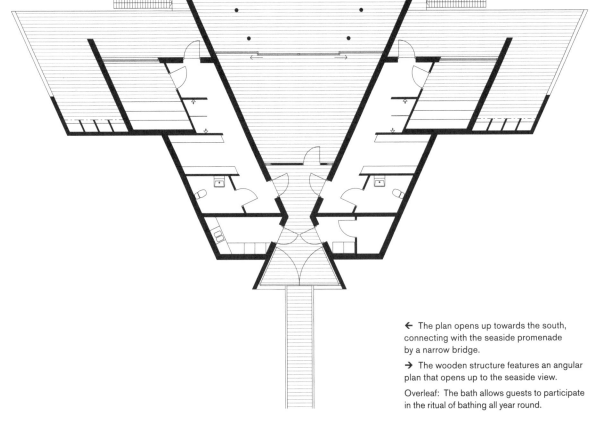

← The plan opens up towards the south, connecting with the seaside promenade by a narrow bridge.

→ The wooden structure features an angular plan that opens up to the seaside view.

Overleaf: The bath allows guests to participate in the ritual of bathing all year round.

Hamra National Park and Crown Jewels

Ljusdal, Sweden
Completed 2013

In 2011 Sweden's Environmental Protection Agency hosted an architecture and design competition for a new graphic and architectonic visual identity for the country's national parks, the aim being to protect, nurture and present the natural wonders to be found there. White's competition entry, a collaboration with the design agency Happy Forsman & Bodenfors, proposed a set of design guidelines for presenting the unique qualities of Swedish national parks. These encompassed advice about the organization of entrance locations, service and guidance functions, plus a suggested kit of design components, comprising furniture, a picnic cottage, observation towers, signs, toilets, barbecues, bear-safe waste disposal and viewing platforms. These all use finely milled local timber with dovetail joints, whitewood boards, concrete and weathering steel grating.

The project's name, 'Crown Jewels', derives from the graphic symbol that marks the location of national parks on the map. The star or snow crystal has become an established symbol in Sweden to denote all protected countryside. Extruded from the two-dimensional symbol to form a three-dimensional object, the star transforms into a crown. Gilded three-dimensional renditions of the crown are dotted about the landscape to indicate the special areas of interest, as well as the inherent wealth of the natural environment.

During the inauguration of Hamra National Park, schoolchildren from Ljusdal acted as forest guides. They were well prepared for the task and generously shared their knowledge about wildlife and plants. Involving the children in the process is one way of future-proofing this rich environment.

↓ Hidden in the forest, the crown with its golden patina is an interesting and mysterious object for discovery.

→ A six-pointed star marks the location of national parks on visitor maps, so we proposed that extruded versions of this symbol be used in situ like noticeboards.

↘ Platforms and furniture in the national park are made of whitewood.

Naturum Vattenriket

Kristianstad, Sweden
Completed 2011

Only a short walk from the city of Kristianstad in Sweden's southern Skåne region, a vast wetland area expands around the Helge river. In the middle of this rich birdland, Naturum Vattenriket rises from the waters, a neat timber palace for experiencing and learning about the unique habitat of the marsh. The Naturum or visitor centre is in a UNESCO biosphere reserve, a model area for interplay between nature and people. The site is so close to the city of Kristianstad that the building can be seen from the main square.

One of more than 30 Naturum buildings around Sweden, this centre is co-funded by the Swedish Environmental Protection Agency and is situated in what was previously a polluted and inaccessible area. It welcomes around 80,000 visitors a year – double the number initially expected – and they are free to explore the wetlands from a variety of perspectives provided by the Naturum for observing wildlife.

Two walkways lead visitors out into the wetlands. At the point where they meet, the western walk rises to form the visitor centre. Pillars, glazed panels and structural solar shading in the form of brise-soleils filter light softly throughout the main space, which contains gallery space, restaurants and conference rooms. The building itself lies 4 metres above normal water level to ensure there is no risk of flooding from the ebb and flow of the Helge river.

The eastern walk is lower and level with the ground, creating a protected, recessed area like a bird's nest in the osier beds. Heat-treated pine used in the façades, and a linseed-oiled boardwalk, ensure that these surfaces are weatherproofed while slowly weathering to silver-grey.

↓ The wetlands are home to a variety of wildfowl, which must be protected from over-exposure. The building was partly designed as a screen between visitors and the lakeside habitat.

→ The pine-clad Naturum is in a beautifully tranquil spot, and the wildlife can be observed from the stepped seating outside.

← The visitor centre sits like a bird's nest among the reeds in the Helge river. From this protected space visitors can get a closer look at the water, native plants and wildlife.

↘ The western façade. From this side of the building, including the roof terrace and the interior, visitors can get a panoramic view of the lake.

↓ The eastern façade. The laminated veneer lumber frame construction provides structural and aesthetic rigour to the building. The timber slats echo those used inside, for everything from ceiling baffles to wall partitions.

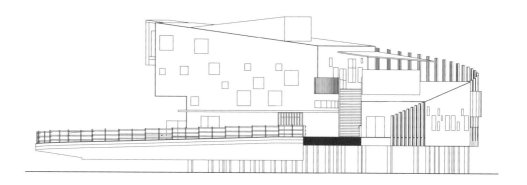

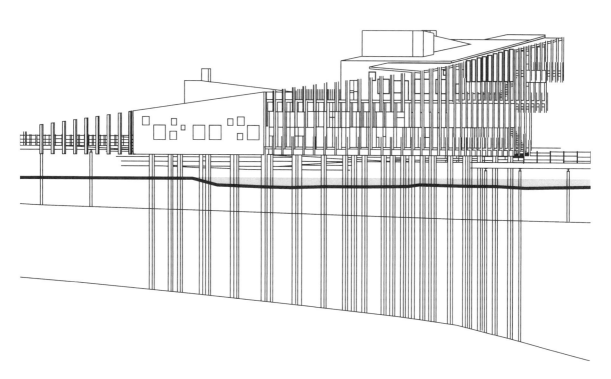

Naturum Oset

Örebro, Sweden
Completion planned 2019

The shores of Lake Hjälmaren form part of a much-loved nature reserve of rolling hills and lakes, but only a couple of decades ago, this was the dirty backwater of Örebro. Naturum Oset is a visitor centre right in the middle of this popular leisure area, and it tells the story of how a forgotten landscape was brought back to life. A century ago Lake Hjälmaren was the site of Sweden's largest landscape project, the objective being to establish new land for agriculture. The project failed and the area became a dumping ground for industrial waste, leaving the lakes in a sad condition. It would take 20 years of landscape restoration to make the Oset-Rynningeviken nature reserve into a healthily functioning habitat.

Naturum Oset is a competition-winning proposal for a visitor centre that reminds people about the area's regeneration, and promotes active local involvement in the protection of the reserve. The building, commissioned by the Swedish Environmental Protection Agency, had to fulfil the strictest rules of sustainable architecture while making the outstanding natural environment accessible to everyone.

Naturum Oset is not one building, but a cluster. The largest of these are partially set into a hillock, yet the distinctive form of the asymmetrical roofs remains visible. The lakes around them will eventually be developed over several levels to sit in harmony with the land. An orangery will replace the old harbour office so that visitors can participate in the cultivation of plants and trees on the hills. Additional overnight visitor pavilions are also planned among the trees, allowing guests to immerse themselves fully in nature.

↓ Profile plan of Naturum Oset, which shows buildings partly set into the hillside. Solar panel roofs unify the appearance of the lakeside buildings.

↙ The Naturum consists of a cluster of buildings on reclaimed land beside what was once a series of heavily polluted lakes. The area is now a verdant and healthy habitat for all kinds of plants and wildlife.

↑ ↓ Timber walkways around the Naturum allow people of all ages and levels of physical fitness to access the lush natural environment, promoting active local involvement in the protection of the reserve.

Naturum Fulufjället

Älvdalen, Sweden
Completed 2003

The national park Fulufjället in the region of Dalarna has
both drama and serenity. Here you can find the highest
waterfall in the country, surrounded by mountain
ranges, canyons, unspoilt woodland and marshes. The
Naturum, commissioned by the Swedish Environmental
Protection Agency, is an educational and inspiring
gateway to this natural environment. The humble timber
building sits unobtrusively in the landscape, while its
interior, clad with wax-finished birch panels, presents
the mighty view outside.

   The brief stipulated that the surroundings must be
accessible by footbridges and paths, and must also
include a location proposal and design exhibition. The
exhibition addresses visitors of all ages and levels of
knowledge, vividly decoding the signs of this particular
landscape type. Visitors learn about the year of the
bear – from spring feeding and breeding to hibernation
– as well as how to tell mountain weather from cloud
formations, and the cycle of the subarctic seasons.
Time is a design factor in the building, which will
weather to grey in years to come. It is tough but
fully degradable so that it could, if necessary, return
to nature, leaving no trace of its presence.

↗ Exhibits are dotted around the interior
in slim cases that can be viewed from both
sides. The large windows give ample daylight.

↓ The building is constructed to have
minimal impact on the site while giving
superb views of the natural world outside.

→ The Naturum sits discreetly within the
ancient, unspoilt landscape. The marshland
directly in front of it is fed by the waterfall.

Kastrup Sea Bath

Tårnby, Denmark
Completed 2005

Imagine the lakeside piers of childhood summers, the warm and familiar surface of the wooden planks as you run barefoot towards the biggest-ever splash. The Kastrup Sea Bath is a built memory of this feeling, an elevated and curved gesture over the water. Its silhouette gradually changes as you move around it. The bath, which is open to the public free of charge at all times, is one of many architectural gems in the Ørestad region of Copenhagen. Conceived as a fully accessible outdoor swimming facility and designed to last for generations, it has transformed a neglected brownfield site into one of Denmark's most enchanting, recognizable and popular leisure destinations for visitors and locals alike.

Inclusivity was an important part of the design concept. All 870 square metres of the wooden deck platform are open to visitors, and it is the ideal place for exercise, play or a peaceful evening swim, irrespective of age and physical mobility. Ramps and other special features make it accessible to everyone.

A wooden pier stretches from the shore to the deck, and curves around to form a circular enclosure. The pier gradually rises above the sea level and ends in a 5-metre diving platform. The circular shape creates a concentrated interior that provides shelter from the wind and the perfect retreat for swimming and sunbathing. A continuous bench runs along the pier, providing additional space for leisure and reflection. At night and during the long, dark winter, dramatic lighting emphasizes the sculptural design. It is constructed from Azobe timber, an African hardwood that was selected for its remarkable longevity and aesthetic qualities. Azobe shares the same lifespan as steel and is resistant to rot and woodworm, ensuring that Kastrup will be enjoyed by many generations of locals and visitors to come.

↓ → The form of this swimming facility, affectionately known as 'The Snail', was conceived in response to the north-facing beach. It provides shelter from the wind and is eqipped with changing rooms, lockers and diving boards.

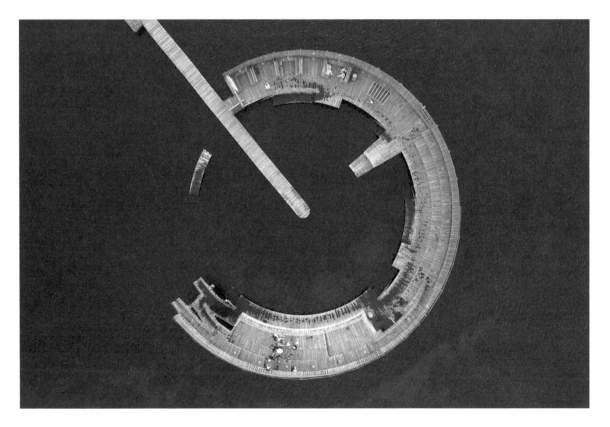

→ Parallel to the pier, a sloping ramp (top) enables wheelchair access to the sea.

↓ A continuous bench runs along the pier, providing additional space for relaxation.

↘ At the tip of the Snail there are three levels of diving platforms and plenty of space for sunbathing.

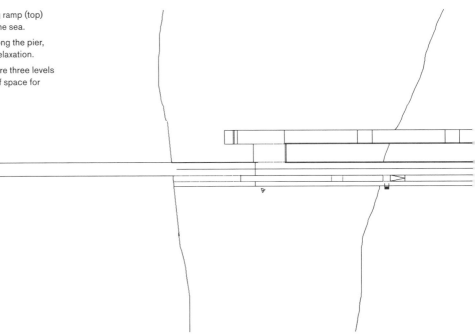

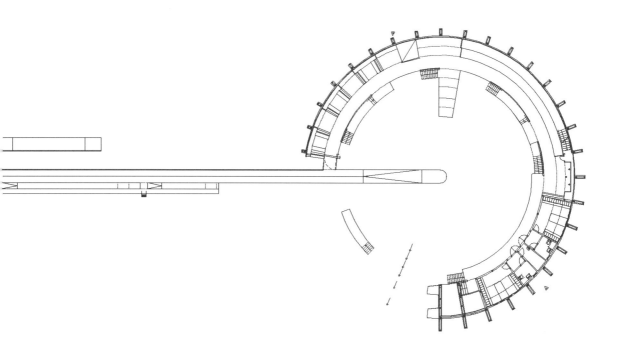

Amber Road Trekking Cabins

Baltic Sea Coastline, Latvia
Competition proposal 2017

The Bee Breeders' Amber Road Trekking Cabin competition called for a design of traveller's cabin suitable for erecting at regular intervals along the Amber Road trekking route, which runs the length of Latvia. The structure had to provide shelter from mosquitoes and all kinds of weather, and defer to the dramatic forest and beach landscape along the route. White's proposal, an exercise in sustainability, was awarded first prize.

The proposal, called 'Link', introduces a series of wooden moles, which are structural piers used as breakwaters along the beach that indicate the location of the cabins. From the moles, narrow tracks lead to the cabins in the forest. These tracks, and the cabins, are made of local timber, which helps to reduce waste and ensures that they will blend in with local architecture over time.

In the centre of the cabin, and open to the sky, is a circular hearth, where trekkers can gather around a fire

to share stories, food and experiences. This space offers views to the landscape and supports a mosquito net during the summer months. Four individual cubicles on each side of the hearth offer privacy, solitude and a view of the surrounding forest.

↓ The rectangular cabin has four cubicles, one in each corner, with the circular open-air hearth in the centre.

→ The cabin is a low-impact building made of local timber and completely in tune with the ecology of the site.

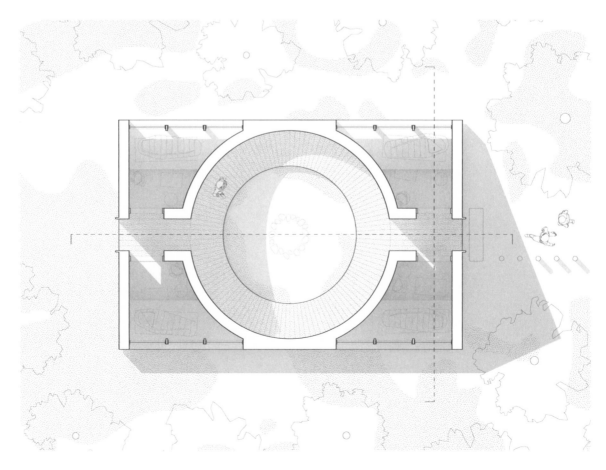

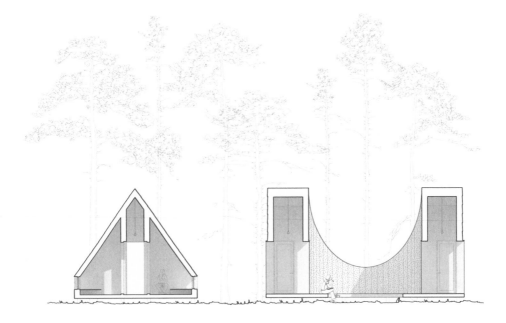

↑ Section of the trekking cabin, with a cubicle on each side of the entrance.

↓ The cabins are found along an anticipated hiking network, transecting the coastal landscape.

↑ → Cross-section through the middle of a cabin, showing the full height above the entrance doors, and the outdoor circular hearth with seating.

↓ The cubicle is the most intimate space of the structure.

In an age when it is not necessary to leave home to be at work, a good workplace has to have a unique appeal. Inspiring spaces that support collaborative creativity and exchange of knowledge start with people being interested in people. Understanding a workplace's requirement to provide a space for colleagues to focus both alone and collaborate as a team helps us design spaces that support the well-being of the employees as well as the environment. Workplaces are important building blocks of towns and cities – our aim is to design them to make a positive contribution to our environment.

The ways we live and work are constantly evolving. Flexible hours, shift work, AI, global collaboration and communication supported by technology mean that workplaces have had to adapt. Being in the same space at the same time has a special value in the digital age. We honour the meeting of people with architecture that promotes the exchange of knowledge and experiences, of focus and activity.

Good interior design caters to functional needs and evokes emotive responses. We work with high-quality, ethical materials that age with grace, repurposing or reusing elements to influence responsible consumption, lower environmental impact and improve health. Consideration of form, light, texture and colour communicates stories that heighten our experience and strengthen our relationship to a place.

MAKE WORK-PLACES THAT WORK

Johanneberg Science Park

Gothenburg, Sweden
Completed 2015

A science park is a transnational and innovative environment that facilitates close contact between education, business and society. The one in Johanneberg, run in partnership between Chalmers University, the City of Gothenburg and 12 companies, gathers 400 people from different parts of business and academia, and it is clear that informal contact between researchers, developers and stakeholders can lead to new research and working teams. To encourage collaboration and meetings, shared areas, such as conference rooms, communication spaces, the café, canteen and entrance spaces, are generously sized. Other bonuses of having shared spaces are lower investment and operating costs, as well as a reduction in energy use. The tenants sign 'green contracts' in which they agree to make minimal environmental impact. As a result, the underground parking garage

is actually designed for bicycles, and includes showers and changing rooms for those who cycle to work.

The science park consists of two buildings connected by a bridge, and both are orientated to get maximum daylight. The window strips are dual-purpose: they offer shade on sunny days, or can be rotated to reflect sunlight back into parts of the building that need it. Green roofs on various levels are excellent for absorbing rainwater. However, most of the surrounding surfaces are water-permeable, so that excess rain can be collected and disposed of in waste-water treatment plants. Another green idea is that materials left over from the construction process have been used for making outdoor furniture. All in all, the buildings of the science park attain the highest levels of ecological, social and economic sustainability.

→ This plan of the fourth floor shows the connecting path between the two buildings. Workplaces are distributed along the façades, and meeting rooms, services and lifts are at the core of the floor plan.

↘ This section shows the fourth-floor connecting bridge and the entrance atrium that stretches from the ground floor to the third floor. The stepped façade gives better daylight conditions.

↓ Located on the campus of Chalmers University, the two buildings are connected via bridges over the main pedestrian route. The façades are comprised completely of window strips, some laminated in gold and others in silver.

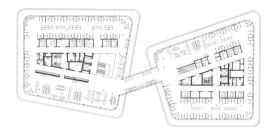

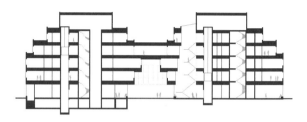

White's Stockholm Office

Stockholm, Sweden
Completed 2003

At the turn of the millennium, when our Stockholm office was outgrowing its studio space in the Old City, it was decided to develop a piece of land – not even a site at that point – and build a new office that would incorporate sustainability in every possible way. The new structure eventually became one of our most future-proof buildings, and we know this because, while using it more than ever, we are still growing into it. With White acting as architect, project manager and future occupant, the office proved to be the perfect test bed for research-led design and engineering. Our primary aim, though, was to create architecture in harmony with structural innovations that reduce energy consumption.

The prize-winning office is simple in form and makes a connection with the historic industrial buildings and warehouses of the area. The urban landscape has a hard-edged character to the north, where the Skanstull bridges extend over the site. Meanwhile, the western and southern sides overlook the Hammarby canal and its locks, and a walkable residential area has been developed to the east. A public footpath and cycle lanes follow the route of

the canal right up to the sunny side of the building, where a pedestrian skybridge connects it to the office entrance, which stands four storeys above the canal.

The office has large floor plates with open-plan areas, where a pleasant acoustic environment has been achieved by using noise-reducing materials. Paint has been used sparingly, and all materials – steel, concrete, glass and timber – are shown in their natural forms. The building's glazed façade is framed by a light metallic structure, and at roof level a receded timber volume houses the canteen and a meeting room. Indoor climate is controlled through the thermal mass of the concrete structure, keeping the office cool in summer while retaining warmth in the colder months. In addition, the building's exposed concrete joists incorporate a cooling system that uses water from the canal. These passive design solutions are complemented by smart technology, such as automated awnings and solar panels, to achieve maximum energy efficiency.

To create an ecologically sound environment, the terrace is planted with herbs, vegetables, shrubs and flowers. Hives, too, are provided for the bees that

pollinate the plants and provide pots of honey that we gratefully collect at the end of the season.

Some large areas of the open-plan workspaces face the canal, while smaller offices and meeting rooms face the steep bank leading up to the bridges. However, the strategic position of the building demands that all its sides be active frontages (for example, the entrances at ground level are almost entirely glazed, exposing all office activity). The office is designed to allow functions and activities within to evolve and change over time to meet different needs, changing methodology and new technology. Its adaptive capacities and approachable character ensure that the building is resilient and will be relevant for decades to come.

↙ A pedestrian skybridge connects the office entrance to Skansbron bridge, the lowest of three bridges that span the canal and connect the north and south of the city.

↓ → The beautifully planted roof garden is a peaceful place for people to have meetings or eat lunch. Every year each employee receives a small pot of honey, very locally produced in the rooftop beehives.

← Even though the building has extensive glazing, exceptionally high environmental standards have been achieved, and energy use is a mere 85 kWh/m²/year. Birchwood flooring adds a touch of warmth to the minimalist interior, which makes maximum use of natural daylight.

↓ The building is situated on a specially constructed dock that was previously open water. It sits away from the edge of the canal, so it is possible to walk along the canal and seaside that reaches all the way along the south of Södermalm island.

Overleaf: The glasshouse that is our office is a familiar sight to all people who pass on the bridge (from which this photo was taken), walk along the seaside path or pass in the boats on the lock just in front.

Façade Design for Optimized Daylighting

ARQ Research Project 2013

Commercial buildings, primarily offices, are generally considered to be energy-intensive, but the design of the Stockholm headquarters of the financial group SEB bucks that trend. The building is a concrete example of a project where evidence-based knowledge was taken on board during the design process, progressing from competition to programme phase. It involved a development process that lasted from 2011 to 2013, and the result was an innovative architectural proposal.

White began by establishing a multidisciplinary team of architects and environmental engineers to undertake the competition, and at an early stage formulated its goals. The first was to minimize solar gain, which can cause overheating during warmer seasons; the second was to maximize daylight and the view towards the waterfront. The design included some key aspects to achieve the best possible daylight autonomy. To begin with, self-shading was applied by inclining the south façade towards the ground and adding rotation to the east–west façades to minimize perpendicular solar rays. After that, we increased the window head-height to maximize daylight penetration. The third strategy was to create three-dimensional angulation of façade elements so that indirect daylight reflections and intermediate light transitions would be diffused. The final strategy was to include atria to allow daylight to penetrate to the core and to street level.

The concept of daylight autonomy led White to define a design scheme that could balance the positive and negative aspects of windows. In architectural research, measuring daylight has become more accurate, with the aim of giving more reliable predictions about the actual performance of the built environment. Dynamic daylight metrics take location, climate and building orientation into consideration, as well as including annualized data. These metrics provide a clear picture of daylight performance, and spatial daylight autonomy data can help architects make good design decisions.

The design scheme was developed using parametric modelling supported by advanced simulation and modelling tools. Apart from the goal strategies already mentioned, the design strategy on which this project mostly relies is the modulation of glazing-to-wall area ratio (GWAR), which is calculated for every floor of the building. This is one of the key parameters determining energy use in office buildings. Excessive windows not only cause much higher energy use, but are also associated with glare, which leads to the wasteful solution of having blinds down while electric lighting is on. Future near-zero-energy office buildings will have a reasonable GWAR to optimize the balance between good daylighting and low heating and cooling loads, while providing a stimulating work environment with satisfying possibilities for window views. White therefore developed innovative façades for the SEB building, using advanced parametric modelling, where GWARs were optimized as a function of orientation.

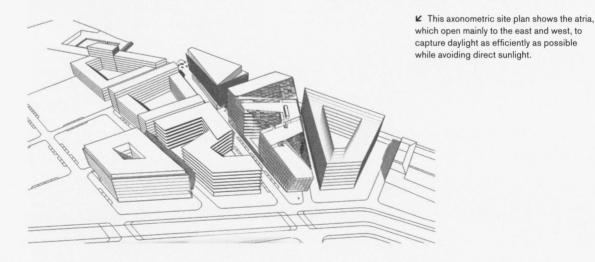

↙ This axonometric site plan shows the atria, which open mainly to the east and west, to capture daylight as efficiently as possible while avoiding direct sunlight.

The roof gardens added to the building's green credentials, while also being pleasant places to meet and relax. Atria were included in the scheme to allow much more light into the workspaces. These would also contribute to decreasing the office block's otherwise high energy consumption.

An important strategy to achieve daylight-optimized design was to diffuse direct sunlight by a three-dimensional angulation of the façade elements.

An Architecture Studio

Kiruna, Sweden
Completed 2015

In 2015 White set up premises in the Arctic mining town of Kiruna in order to be on site for our biggest urban planning assignment – the relocation of the whole town (see p.56). The sign on the door of what was previously a corner shop says simply Ett Arkitektkontor (An Architecture Studio), and it provides a cosy meeting place for architects and locals to discuss the progress of the move, or express any concerns about it.

In choosing the familiar setting of a shop as our office, we hoped to encourage passers-by to pop in for a coffee and a chat with the design team and with one another. That has, in fact, been very successful and the studio has become a community hub, where residents can browse drawings and reading material, and take an active part in the changes that are being planned.

A key strategy in the design plan for the new Kiruna is to reclaim, recycle and reuse materials and cultural artefacts from the old town. Most of this will take place through an upcycling and recycling facility called Kirunaportalen, and it will have several benefits: apart from reducing waste and expense, it will preserve familiar town artefacts that would otherwise have been lost, thus retaining at least some vestiges of the town's original culture and identity.

White's proposal for the new Kiruna is based on a 100-year perspective and embodies an understanding of the geological, social and cultural layers that make the place a home. White's local studio is a small indication of the changes that will take the town towards something completely different, yet strangely familiar.

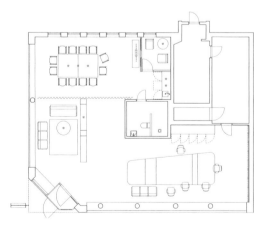

↑ Plan of the office interior. The adjustable table is visible bottom right, and to the left is a relaxed lounge with a meeting room above.

↑ The interior is composed of locally sourced or donated objects that have been retrofitted, reused or upcycled (above).

↑ The office's position on the street corner easily catches the eye of passers-by, while the large shop windows reveal the inviting and unintimidating interior.

↑ This model of the table below shows the possible adjustments in height.

↓ Tthe centrepiece of the office is a purpose-built table that mechanically undulates to form a hill and a valley, or a standing desk and a seating table. As well as being a place to gather around, the table becomes an allegory of the volatile ground conditions of a mining town.

↑ An example of locally upcycled furniture: a pair of armchairs set on a wheeled base.

P5 Väven

Umeå, Sweden
Completed 2015

The P5 conference centre is on the fifth floor of the award-winning Väven Cultural Centre in the heart of Umeå. Situated on the bank of the Umeälven river and surrounded by an Arctic wonderland, the Väven building itself is a hub for Nordic art, music and literature, and P5 is a beacon of activity within it. The conference centre is designed to accommodate many events simultaneously. Consequently, its furnishings, lighting and technology have been chosen to move easily, and be rearranged and adapted to new conditions. Flexibility is embedded throughout the design, but is seamless and invisible to visitors.

The venue offers both a tactile and a sensory experience that characterizes the Northern spirit of homeliness. A crackling firepit warms the entrance hall, where walls of undulating black glass encase the lobby and meeting rooms. The social areas are lined with exquisite wood panelling composed of square blocks of birchwood interwoven with remarkable precision. The rich textures and colours of the interior reference Sami craftsmanship and a love of natural materials, including timber, leather, birch bark, silver and wool.

→ The interior of the P5 conference centre glows with hospitable warmth. The soft, undulating forms and furnishings can accommodate all kinds of meeting.

↘ The birchwood panelling on some of P5's walls is a stunning piece of detailing that echoes the local craft tradition of birch-bark weaving. Apart from their visual impact, the panels add a tactile element to the design and an acoustic intimacy.

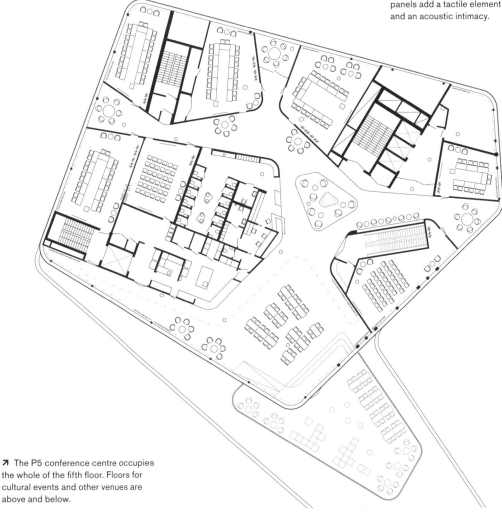

↗ The P5 conference centre occupies the whole of the fifth floor. Floors for cultural events and other venues are above and below.

Oslo Government Centre

Oslo, Norway
Competition proposal 2015

After the government buildings in central Oslo were severely damaged in the July 2011 terror attack, Norway made a decision to move its 6,000 officials into one city-centre location. The aim was to integrate a new government quarter into the heart of the city, thus rebuilding trust among citizens and restoring their sense of safety. Above all, it had to celebrate freedom in the face of adversity.

In a selective competition, the Norwegian Directorate of Public Construction invited six architectural practices to submit designs. The need for security in a densely built urban environment was paramount, but, rather than creating new boundaries and separations, White's proposal takes a radical approach that actively breaks down the historical, cultural and physical barriers of the city. To this end, entrances are strategically placed on the streets, making them both destinations and meeting places. The transparent ground floor signals confidence in the building and lets in as much natural light as possible in order to create healthy, productive spaces and minimize the need for artificial lighting. Høyblokka, the main government building that was damaged in the terror attack, would remain the tallest building in the

area. Within the government quarter, new workplace strategies are proposed to increase collaboration, and social spaces have been introduced. Our design for the Oslo Government Centre provides a great opportunity to improve the quality of urban life, while promoting social coherence and sustainability.

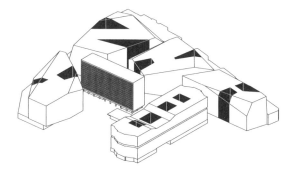

↓ ↑ The various shapes of the quarter reflect the organic structure of the surrounding city, and incorporate the natural ways of moving across the site.

→ The generous space and public seating between the buildings create a sense of an 'urban living room' with vivid street life.

Epidemic Sound

Stockholm, Sweden
Completed 2015

The music company Epidemic Sound acquired the
floor below its attic loft in an old brewery building in
central Stockholm, and took the opportunity to redesign
and reinforce both its company identity and its work
process. The stairwells are a visual as well as functional
link between the floors. The office space is largely
open-plan, but is complemented by closed spaces for
meetings and bespoke listening booths. Ceilings have
been stripped of their cladding to reveal the functions
beneath, and the second-hand furniture has been
chosen to resonate with the industrial character of
the building.

The overall design is robust and rough, and
pays great attention to the acoustic qualities of the
space. The expanded office area is an innovative and
productive place to work, entirely in accord with the
company's identity.

↓ ↑ The industrial character is complemented by
bright steel stairs and recycled furniture.

Transformer Station

Uppsala, Sweden
Completed 2009

This transformer, which transforms voltage from high to low and sends it to a network of smaller substations, provides the entire centre of Uppsala with electricity. Located in a former industrial area that has gradually become more residential, the facility was not designed to meet the eyes of an emerging neighbourhood, but moving it would have been a complex and costly affair. It therefore had to stay put and, to meet ever-increasing demand for electricity, have structures added to it. For this reason, the architectural solution had to accommodate new volumes and also provide space for future expansion.

The solution was to enclose the whole complex in metal mesh, reminiscent of a Faraday cage. The tilted orientation of the mesh structure shifts with the perspective of passers-by, and its appearance also varies with daylight and over the seasons. Climbing plants clamber over the façades and roof, transforming the former eyesore into a green feast for the eye.

↓ The weathering steel mesh cage surrounding the transformer has a strong but pleasing presence. It successfully unites the new elements on the site with the original 1960s architecture.

UR Educational Broadcasting Company

Stockholm, Sweden
Completed 2011

Materiality and tactility permeate this project, reflecting the educational values of UR, the Swedish Educational Broadcasting Company. The aim of the design was to create a building that has the same clear, open attitude as UR itself, and this has given rise to a simplicity in materials and form that will age with dignity.

The challenge was to create a unique, flexible workspace for a diverse and agile organization. We started by adding a limited new volume on top of UR's existing two-storey building to meet the need for new light and open spaces that would complement the refurbished studios. The main staircase connects all three floors and allows spontaneous encounters among colleagues.

White acted as lead consultant and was responsible for the entire process, from brief and planning process

to coordinating all consultants during the design period. We worked in close collaboration with UR, holding discussions that informed the brief and the building's functions, and that helped us to convey the identity of the company. This allowed the White team to develop a clear idea of how to tackle the design.

The scale of the building had to work with the duality encountered on site – nineteenth-century buildings in the park to the south, and a 1960s TV studio block to the north. It was therefore decided to incorporate elements from both eras in our choice of materials. On the side that faces the 1960s structure, the roof and façade are clad in aluminium. The façade on the other side is clad in plywood, which gives a warmer look and works with the smaller scale of the old buildings.

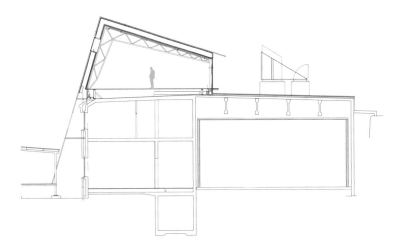

← The new workspace wraps around the old building like a shell that forms the new top floor, and visually unites all the floors of the building.

↙ ↓ The materials used in the extension include plywood and aluminium, providing colourful interior details for common areas.

↗ The asymmetrical extension is a substantial yet subtle addition to the building on which it sits. The design maximizes light.

↘ The ground-floor terrace.

Quality Hotel Globen Event Hall

Stockholm, Sweden
Completed 2014

In the arena district of south Stockholm, visitor numbers and the demand for hotel facilities are increasing, and this led the Quality Hotel Globen to commission a new lobby with an event hall for private functions. The aim was to create a multi-purpose event space that would suit many different audiences and convey a feeling of celebration. The development network Dsearch, part of White Research Lab, used advanced modelling to design the cladding for the hall and saw it through to factory delivery. In fact, computational design thinking was embedded from early concept development to final fabrication, and the resulting space provides guests with a variety of effects that change according to viewpoint and time of day.

The volume has visually performative architecture – hundreds of unique rigid lamellae make up the façades, arranged in eight systems that overlap and intersect to distort the cube geometry. The cutting scheme for the lamellae was digitally controlled to minimize the use of materials. An LED lighting system is embedded in the ribbed cladding structure and can be programmed to suit whatever activities and gatherings take place in the versatile event hall.

↓ The suspended volume and its changing visual performance are best experienced from the escalators.

→ The drawing shows how the event space sits above the lobby that connects the banquet hall to the existing hotel.

↘ & Overleaf: An integrated lighting system works with the ribbed structure to provide ever-changing visual effects.

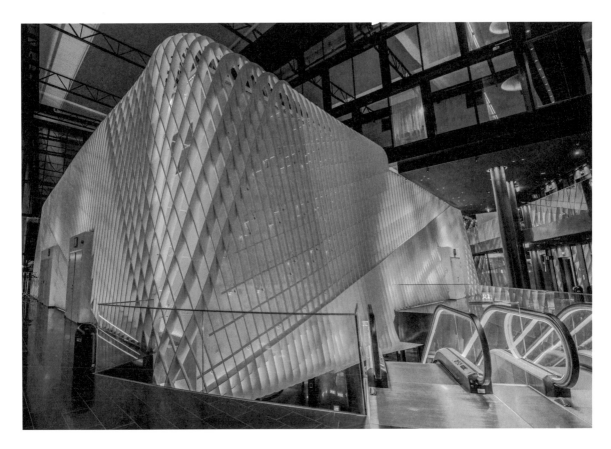

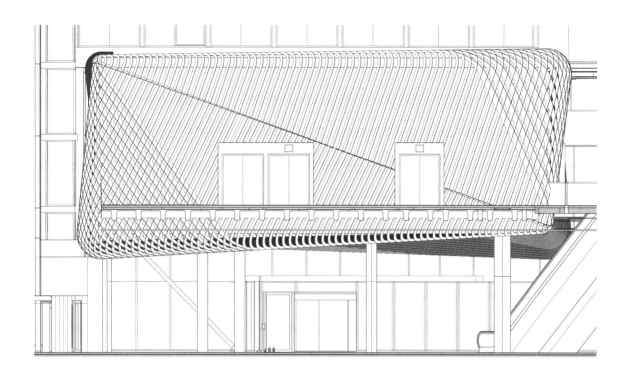

Växjö City Hall and Central Station

Växjö, Sweden
Competition proposal 2016

The city of Växjö began investigating ways to improve its urban infrastructure in response to projected population growth, an increase in tourism and a desire to build on its reputation as a leading European green city. The ambition was to develop a new civic hub and council offices to replace the existing town hall, which was no longer fit for purpose, and to expand the capacity of the railway-station building. Following an open competition, a radical proposal was selected – a combined town hall and railway station to meet the needs of the 90,000 people living in the city.

The juxtaposition of the two facilities in a 24-hour space means that local citizens, visitors, city officials and their callers are always passing through. The six-storey town hall has been designed as an exemplary workplace to improve the health, happiness and productivity of the 600 council employees. Visitor experience and the needs of different travelling groups informed the station design, which has waiting rooms, shops, restaurants and other services. An important part of the scheme was to increase accessibility to the city centre, so a public footbridge at first-floor level now connects with both sides of the railway. At street level there is a new park and a square, and a proposed planted canopy walkway will eventually connect all elements of the hub.

The central location of the building calls out for a strong identity, and the stakes are high in the 'greenest city in Europe'. The tilted façade reduces the total exterior surface and thus permanently reduces energy costs. The material selection is locally rooted: glass, a product of the region; wood from the vast forests of Småland; and local stone. The building's wooden structure is clad with a mixture of opaque and transparent coloured shingles. Some of these are electricity-generating solar cells, while others provide shade and reveal or conceal parts of the wooden façade. The timber construction frames all the functions of the building in a warm embrace, and the new complex has been awarded Sweden's highest certification of sustainability.

↓ A cross-section shows the six storeys of the building, with a courtyard at the bottom.

↗ The sloping façades of the building reduce the surface area and therefore energy wastage.

→ An outdoor walkway leads to the various train platforms, all on the level below.

↘ Serving both the town hall and the railway station, the building, framed by soothing wood panelling, is designed for intensive use.

Täby Municipal Hall

Täby, Sweden
Completed 2017

The new municipal hall in Täby is an open and welcoming space. All meetings between residents and the municipality take place at the entrance level. A prominent reception also functions as an activity information and support centre and help desk for Täby residents. The building is strategically located on the esplanade, which connects the city centre, the library, the church, the swimming pool and the upper secondary school. The space between the municipal hall and the library provides an intimate entrance square.

A ring of rooms for meetings, relaxation and communal use are located around the central atrium. Outside this ring of rooms there are spaces for other types of activity including larger gathering spaces, places for reflection, project rooms and resource rooms. Set back from the roof is the penthouse, a separate space for internal gatherings, which houses a dining space, a kitchen and an exercise area.

The façade consists of a glass system with structural glazing for maximum transparency and openness. To prevent insolation and to create character, the building has been fitted with external sun protection slats made of brass, which from a life-cycle perspective has a very low carbon footprint. Täby Municipal Hall is designed with the highest aim in sustainability, creating a new democratic heart for the inhabitants of the city.

↓ Loacted near the hospital in an area previously used for parking, the municipal hall is a relaxed space for residents and the municipality to meet.

↗ Cross section.

↘ Floor plan, level 6.

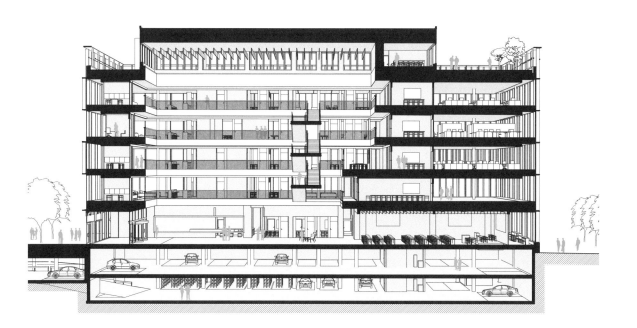

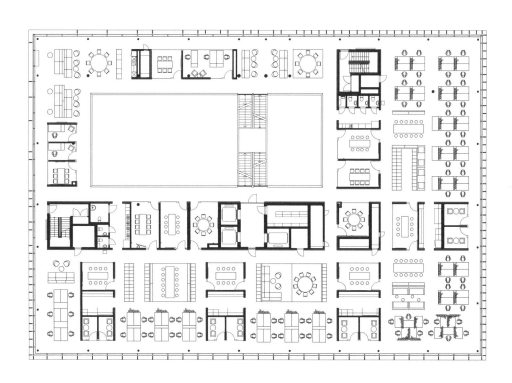

Swedish Energy Agency

Eskilstuna, Sweden
Completed 2017

When the Swedish Energy Agency (Energimyndigheten) moved into new premises in an old foundry, fresh thinking guided the design process towards a healthy and inspiring workplace. While preserving the legacy of the foundry space, traces of which are beautifully incorporated into the new design, the agency needed a more efficient office that would promote creativity and motion to result in a healthy working environment. With a gentle push into the twenty-first century, the office was transformed into a workplace that supports the 350 staff members with different functional zones and a playful character.

Reuse has been a major part of the project. As much as 73 per cent of the office furniture was reused from the agency's previous premises, upcycled for a second life and incorporated into the new building's revitalizing colour scheme. The agency has a very flexible workforce, often based at other locations,

and sometimes gathering in larger numbers. The solution was a hybrid office, offering a variety of spaces such as quiet rooms, common areas and open-plan offices in different zones.

Throughout the building is a route of activities that promote play and physical exercise, such as a climbing wall, gymnastics rings and a swing, as well as lounge areas. This route snakes through the office and allows employees and guests to work out, take a break or host a walk-and-talk meeting.

→ Spontaneous activity is encouraged with swings and exercise equipment.

↓ A soft colour scheme and natural materials create a warm and textured atmosphere, together with exposed building materials, such as concrete and bricks.

The Hub

Uppsala, Sweden
Completed 2017

Uppsala Science Park is recognized as one of the best incubators for scientific and technological innovation in the world. Until recently, there was no natural meeting point within the park for Uppsala's creative community, which has received international acclaim for its progress in the fields of life sciences, biotech, medicine and IT. The Hub is a highly anticipated space for innovation and meetings, with a warm, welcoming character.

The architectural challenge was to design a building with a strong character that harmonized with its context and provided flexible space for a complex set of activities. The atrium reaches right through the five floors of the cubic building. The organic surge of the atrium is a vertical spine in the building that facilitates social interaction: the balconies and stairs allow spontaneous gatherings and meetings between professions, work cultures and processes.

The façade features a toned terrazzo and large, well-proportioned windows, and colourful fibre cement scales reflect the earthy nuances of the surrounding historical buildings in shades of ochre and umber. The south entrance faces a generous public square, which emphasizes the central role of the building and the communal life it brings to Uppsala Science Park.

The building was nominated as Sweden's Building of the Year in 2018. Its success is the result of a remarkable collaborative process that benefited from the knowledge of fifty entrepreneurs working towards completion within both time and budget.

↓ The welcoming entrance from the south-facing public square is the first part of a building whose main task is to bring people together to create new knowledge.

→ The sculptural staircase creates a continuous space, an undulating wave of wooden rods that frame the warm atmosphere of the atrium.

↘ The interior terraces are natural meeting places. The offices are lit from the atrium light as well as the daylight.

The architecture of the healing environment plays a central role in the process of recovery, for all who spend time there – patients as well as caregivers. Our focus is to design healing environments that reduce stress, increase mobility and strengthen recovery. Our architecture is a result of a deep understanding of human needs and new technology. We benefit from long experience of building for healthcare and draw on decades of evidence-based research into well-being and patient recovery. Thanks to evidence-based design, this knowledge has been transferred from architects to institutions, and beyond.

Building for the community means committing to long-term sustainability. The great investment in healthcare buildings is often a substantial opportunity to add quality to the surrounding infrastructure as well as create a new meeting place for the community, indoors as well as outdoors. We extend the health-promoting perspective well beyond the healthcare building and its surroundings, as promoting health is a principle that permeates the entire practice of architecture and architectural planning.

Our healthcare architecture is future-proofed by spatial planning that allows flexibility and design with the capacity to adapt and reconfigure. Health environments are big investments in society, and, as healthcare is an intensive field of research and development, they are changing at a faster pace than their buildings. Architecture needs to be forward-looking to accommodate changes, and to ensure that the healthcare environment has continuous value for all who spend time there; the beauty of a tree seen through a window, sunlight finding its way in, the grain of wood under your fingertips. We aim to create healthcare architecture that is both sensitive and sensible, and trust the physical environment to be part of the healing process.

DESIGN FOR CARE AND HEALING

Aabenraa Psychiatric Hospital

Aabenraa, Denmark
Completed 2015

Praised for its social and environmental sustainability, this hospital project has a groundbreaking design that contributes to the destigmatization of psychiatric treatment. The aim underpinning the overall plan was to provide a more open and healing environment for such treatment.

The design of this 115-room psychiatric clinic offers patients of all ages a feeling of safety, yet also promotes contact with the outside world. The main building forms a central spine from which seven treatment sections radiate in two starburst formations. This arrangement gives each treatment area a view of the surrounding landscape, while the more intimate outdoor areas between the buildings are designed as lush courtyards and active spaces for exterior treatment cycles. The new clinic and the existing hospital buildings are linked functionally while maintaining their respective identities.

Patients can move around the building freely, and it provides a safe and calm environment for both them and the staff. Rethinking the psychiatric treatment facility has led to an architecture that speaks as softly to its surroundings as it does to its patients.

↓ The layout of the building, with its ray-like clinics projecting from a central spine, encourages social interaction.

→ Plenty of daylight, music rooms, access to gardens and a connection with the landscape were key considerations in the design.

↘ The low-rise clinic has a welcoming atmosphere by both day and night.

←↑ Environmental initiatives are in complete harmony with the interior. Daylight takes priority, and artificial light sources are chosen for aesthetics as well as energy efficiency. Natural green walls absorb noise, while also providing a soothing organic environment.

↗→ Interior and exterior spaces support social interaction during all stages of treatment. Consultations take place in small, quiet rooms, but generously sized spaces are available for group exercise, and the auditorium offers a range of events.

Östra Hospital Emergency Psychiatry Ward

Gothenburg, Sweden
Completed 2006

An emergency psychiatric ward might have locked doors, but that does not mean the architecture itself has to be confined. In fact, psychiatric care requires the architecture to create a free and open atmosphere, breaking down any preconceptions that people may have of institutional environments.

Östra Hospital's emergency ward offers patients, medical staff, relatives and visitors an opportunity to benefit from a welcoming environment that incorporates careful gradations of social character – from the individual bedrooms to seating areas inspired by the vernacular Swedish veranda. Evidence-based research suggests that successful care requires the gradual increase of patients' personal space from their room to the garden, to the wider public realm, with an eventual return to life outside. That is what this hospital provides. It gives patients a sense of continuity in everyday life, whether that is just a view of a tree from their window, or access to a garden without staff escort; these things are vital parts of the healing environment.

The wards are built around three cornerstones in the design concept: the heart, the garden and the group. At the core of each ward is the heart, a sort of open-plan communal area, with living room, kitchen and activity room all grouped around a small glazed conservatory inspired by the design of the traditional Swedish veranda. Within that relaxed space is seating for four or five patients staying in the adjacent rooms. This arrangement results in a corridor-free ward, which makes the building feel less institutional.

The second design cornerstone, the garden, is a sheltered oasis that patients require no escort to visit; in fact, some bedrooms open directly on to it. Open access is actually the essence of this patient-centred design, providing healing spaces with as few restrictions as possible, and offering options from complete privacy to social interaction.

The third and final cornerstone of the design is the group, and the rooms in each ward form a group or patient community. Each patient's room offers various possibilities for solitude, rest and relaxation. The garden is visible from the bed, and a comfortable chair provides a snug place to read, while also offering views over the garden or the communal spaces. This means that the patient's personal sphere can gradually enlarge until they want to engage in the social sphere of the conservatory.

The healing environment aims to be more homely than institutional in character, with a free and open atmosphere. It looks at things from the patient's perspective, offering a dignified environment with overview instead of surveillance. The success of this approach demonstrates the importance of architecture in achieving good results in psychiatric treatment.

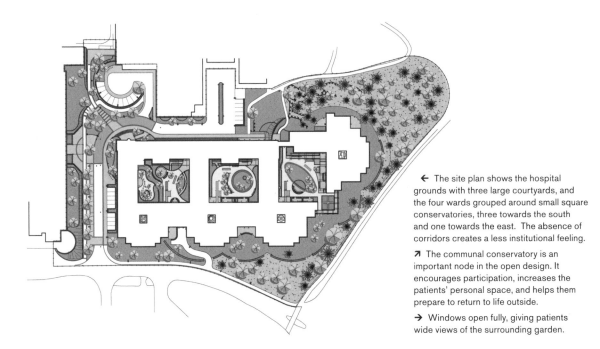

← The site plan shows the hospital grounds with three large courtyards, and the four wards grouped around small square conservatories, three towards the south and one towards the east. The absence of corridors creates a less institutional feeling.

↗ The communal conservatory is an important node in the open design. It encourages participation, increases the patients' personal space, and helps them prepare to return to life outside.

→ Windows open fully, giving patients wide views of the surrounding garden.

Forensic Psychiatry with a Human Face

ARQ Research Project 2012

Rågården is an enclosed space, yet created with an open mind and a sound confidence in the patients' potential for rehabilitation. Its architectural ambition is to unite forensic psychiatry's two objectives: to care for and to guard. The question of how society should deal with disturbed individuals when they break the law is complicated. The matter has been studied for over 70 years, and the findings have varied. It is likely that no single solution will ever be found that best addresses all the different forms of psychiatric problem.

At the time of writing, there are 25 inpatient forensic psychiatric facilities in Sweden caring for barely a thousand patients. Roughly the same number of people receive outpatient care. Of the 200 new patients admitted to psychiatric hospitals every year, the majority (80 per cent) are men. The average length of stay is five years, and is long in comparison with prison sentences for the same crimes. About half the patients have been diagnosed as psychotic, but many are diagnosed with more than one illness, including addiction and personality disorders. An on-site county administrative court determines whether a patient is allowed to leave the building, grants leaves of absence, approves transitions to outpatient care, and eventually releases patients from care. The length of stays in forensic psychiatric care facilities places particularly heavy demands on the content and quality of the care given. This project is guided by the principle that the most seriously ill need the best care.

Rågården, which is located in the outskirts of Gothenburg, was completed in 2013. It has been extensively researched and analysed in terms of how architecture can serve as a tool for faster and better rehabilitation. Research conducted in recent decades appears to demonstrate that architecture does indeed have the potential to provide healing effects, and this makes the work of designers more interesting and more meaningful. During the research process, both staff and patients expressed a desire for the architecture to feel residential, like a home rather than an institution, giving the patients a feeling of control and coherence. A shared vision ultimately emerged through the work of planning the building, with care routines and building design proceeding in unison.

As we learnt at Östra Hospital (see p.224), closed psychiatric wards have locked doors, but this does not mean that the architecture cannot have a sense of openness. Security is essential, but should not feel oppressive or aggravate the patients. The right architecture works as medicine, creating a free and open atmosphere, and breaking down any preconceptions that people may have about forbidding institutional environments. That ward includes specific design features that help to reduce stress and aggressive behaviour. These include single-patient bedrooms with private toilets and showers, good acoustic design, extensive daylight, access to a garden and floor plans that facilitate good observation by staff but balance safety with patient dignity. Rågården is an enclosed space created with an open mind.

Architecture serves an as important tool for faster and better rehabilitation. Physical exercise in the pool or gym, the wider view and contact with the outside world, as well as private contemplation or spiritual relief, are just as important for recovering the mind as is medical care.

Rågården is an enclosed space
created with an open mind,
designed in collaboration with staff
and patients to facilitate faster and
better rehabilitation.

Hóspital Simón Bolívar

Bogotá, Colombia
Design proposal 2015

As one of the best clinics in Latin America, Hóspital Simón Bolívar cares for people who come from near and far, and has a significant socio-economic value to the community. The clinic, which specializes in treating burns, needs to double in size as well as capacity, growing from its present site without changing its footprint and without closing down during construction. Architects and social sustainability experts at White therefore joined the local expertise on site to pool knowledge about healthcare architecture. Our contribution to the process has been to work with the medical staff and hospital management in order to devise ways of maintaining services with minimal disruption and optimized logistics. White has arranged workshops and study internships, resulting in deeper understanding of the needs of the organization, and strategies for change.

The hospital staff and management are dedicated to maintaining a level of excellence while undergoing all the necessary improvements to sustainable infrastucture, function and comfort. To this end, the new addition will replace the existing hospital in stages. The surface area, developed from an evidence-based design concept, will be doubled. The overall building is designed as a single volume, featuring a green terrace façade specifically adjusted to the local climate. The goal is to integrate the hospital into the local community of northern Bogotá, contributing to the social sustainability of the area. The project will be a collaborative manifestation of healthcare expertise within both medicine and architecture.

↓ The entire site has been increased in density to accommodate the ambitious building programme, as regulations prevent any extension beyond its boundaries.

↗ Green spaces are found throughout the hospital and its grounds. Each responds to specific micro-climatic conditions and is designed to provide the most suitable ecosystem benefits for that area.

→ New patient rooms are accommodated in the tower volume that will occupy the current arrival forecourt.

↘ At basement level, there is a separate thoroughfare, with cycle path, for car and ambulance access, which allows safer and more efficient access. The ground-floor main entrance opens on to a vehicle-free plaza that becomes a more peaceful public space.

Radiation Therapy Centre

Lund, Sweden
Completed 2013

For safety reasons, the equipment used for radiation treatment has conventionally been installed and used underground, which means that patients have often been treated in bunker-like rooms without daylight or exterior views. By rethinking the architecture, it has been made possible to locate the Radiation Therapy Centre in central Lund in a building that is saturated by daylight.

An innovative architectural layout allows improved function without compromising security. Access to daylight is better for everyone, staff and patients alike, but the above-ground location also makes it easier to undertake the frequent technical maintenance the equipment requires. The architectural solution to ensuring safety was to position the equipment so that it is concentrically shielded by a sequence of walls, ensuring that the radiation is contained and controlled in all directions from the source. In addition, construction techniques and material choices were revised and tested. The latter included finding new concrete formulas to ensure radiation absorption.

As part of Skåne University Hospital's oncology unit, this clinic connects with the older clinic next door via a shared entrance hall. Centrally located atria bring extra daylight into both. The most important objective for the new oncology unit was to help patients facing the trauma of cancer to have their treatment in a calm and pleasant environment. Integrated into the ceilings of the radiotherapy rooms are light installations that form a colourful kaleidoscope of patterns, designed by the Swedish artist Aleksandra Stratimirovic. The constantly undulating sequence of light is an 'ornament in motion' that provide a soothing distraction to help scatter the shadows in the mind.

↓ The Radiation Therapy Centre has become a vivid landmark thanks to the colourful mosaic cladding in shimmering glass. This façade cleverly conceals the complexity and challenges of the construction.

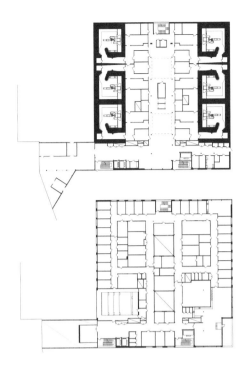

↑ Level 1 plan (top), displaying the wall thickness required for radiation safety. Level 4 plan (above), with patient rooms that require privacy but not radiation protection.

→ Central atria flood the interiors with light. The bright openness is also intended to inspire confidence in patients.

↓ The colourful façade panels create an interesting play of light, during day and night.

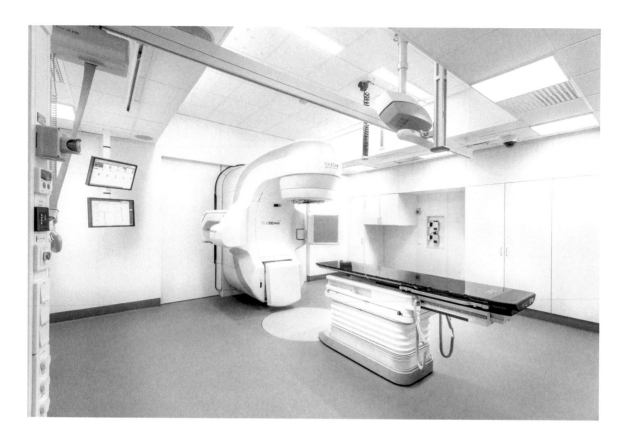

↑ The radiotherapy treatment rooms are a tech-intensive environment, yet in this innovative oncological treatment ward, the rooms are situated above ground, and connect directly to bright spaces with daylight.

↗ Light and colour are hugely important elements, not least in the façade. The result is a friendly building with a calm and welcoming atmosphere.

→ Integrated into the atrium ceilings are light installations forming a kaleidoscope of patterns, designed by the artist Aleksandra Stratimirovic.

Hocus Focus:
Creating a brighter hospital experience

White Research Lab 2014

How can interiors help to shift people's focus from the anxiety of being in a hospital environment? A research team at White, specializing in interior architecture and lighting, developed a design that aimed to achieve this for the paediatric ward at Queen Silvia's Children's Hospital. The main objective was to make a child-friendly space that would mute both the dominance of clinical equipment and the institutional feel of the surroundings. In dialogue with medical staff, patients, parents and relatives, the architects learnt about the children's favourite places. The result was an interior decorated with images of the seasons and lighting schemes that featured many calming focal points.

The first stage of implementing the design involved creating a hygienic base. A framework was then added to accommodate existing functions, such as the play zone, and a gallery wall for the children's drawings incorporated into the waiting room. All the furniture was chosen with consideration of how easily it is disinfected.

The architects aimed at a design that would work for very young children as well as for teenagers, so a playful theme develops throughout the space, aiming to make the technical and medical equipment less frightening. The walls of the waiting room, for example, depict a park in the spring, while the sample rooms show a sunny meadow and a day at the beach.

Design features are deliberately placed to be visible from outside the door of each room, thus arousing the patient's curiosity before they enter, and shifting their thoughts to more pleasant things than treatment. The beach sample room, for instance, greets its young visitors with a pink flamingo, and the lighting inside the room is designed as a sunny embrace. Strong light is required when taking samples, so the upper part of the walls is white, but a dimmer switch has been installed to create a more restful ambience after the treatment. In the summer meadow room, the wall paintings depict swaying grass, and include little surprises visible from various perspectives. For example, a bird-house light can be seen from the treatment chair, and when lying down, children can rest their eyes on the ceiling, where the canopy of a tree is dotted with fibre-optic lights to create the illusion of sunlight filtering through the foliage. Such things offer alternative points of focus that might go some way towards relieving patients' anxiety.

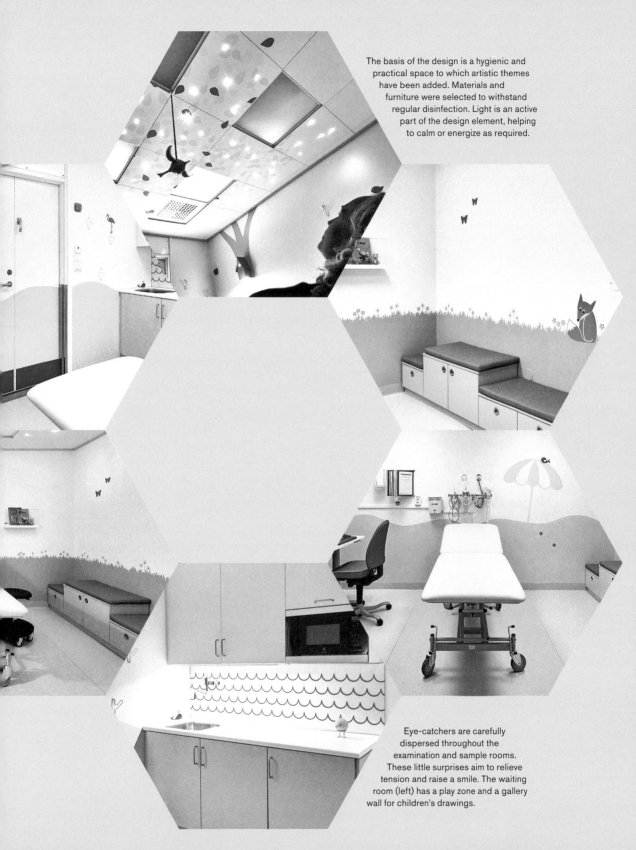

The basis of the design is a hygienic and practical space to which artistic themes have been added. Materials and furniture were selected to withstand regular disinfection. Light is an active part of the design element, helping to calm or energize as required.

Eye-catchers are carefully dispersed throughout the examination and sample rooms. These little surprises aim to relieve tension and raise a smile. The waiting room (left) has a play zone and a gallery wall for children's drawings.

Linköping University Hospital

Linköping, Sweden
Completed 2016

Hospital design in Scandinavia embraces all aspects of health, not just for patients, but for staff, visitors and environment too. Internal and external development of Linköping University Hospital has created a welcoming civic building that is more efficient and actively contributes to its neighbourhood. A new central communication hall with atrium is a striking addition, and artwork is integrated into the structure in line with the principles defined early in the process by a multidisciplinary team. Workflow between departments has also improved thanks, for example, to a new link connecting the hospital to education and research facilities.

Linköping University Hospital has always been fortunate to occupy a central urban location, but its 1970s buildings were neither welcoming nor particularly accessible. The new design has improved this by creating a second entrance that opens on to a new central plaza, where hospital visitors can easily access public transport. Operational efficiency and safety were increased by moving the emergency department to the west side of the building and giving it a dedicated access road, and by providing a lift connection to the rooftop heliport.

The alterations to the hospital campus have also enabled the development and regeneration of the surrounding neighbourhoods. The hospital architecture has therefore had a healing influence on the city outside as well as on the patients within.

↓ The interior plaza is a generous atrium that forms a defined central zone. Large-scale art installations are integrated into the atrium's architecture at ceiling and floor level, and along the walls.

→ The hospital, located in central Linköping, forms part of an attractive, connected neighbourhood.

House of Heroes

Umeå, Sweden
Completed 2017

Intended to ease the rehabilitation process for children suffering from cancer, House of Heroes is designed as a home away from home, an uplifting environment free from white coats and unpleasant treatments. Family support is essential for children with a long-term illness, so the design aims to provide for that by all means possible. It allows parents and children to stay together in a homely environment where the focus is on easing the mind and helping recovery. In this case, architecture can clearly be seen to have a direct and beneficial impact on well-being.

The main focus of the project has been to create a consistently playful environment where young patients and their families can focus on healing. Recreational facilities include a park, complete with duck pond and playground, and adults and children get great enjoyment from them.

House of Heroes sits adjacent to a building that dates from 1913 and was originally the home of the hospital caretaker. The new, purpose-built accommodation contains small apartments with cooking facilities, and these are arranged around a communal activity room where new friends become extended family. A two-storey glass atrium links the old and the new buildings, creating an indoor courtyard with a tree planted in the middle. The building is a glue-laminated construction, clad with Tricoya panels with a perforated pattern. The materials are chosen for their sound and sustainable qualities to make a house fit for heroes.

→ Activity rooms with a variety of toys and games provide happy respite for the recovering children and their families. In this house it is easy to make new friends, which is of great psychological support for the parents and children alike. The rooms provide temporary living arrangements for friends and family so that children are able to recover in a home-like situation.

↓ The old building has been refurbished and now connects via an atrium to the new accommodation block. Both old and new parts focus on community, sustainability and comfort.

New Mother and Child Unit, Panzi Hospital

Bukavu, Democratic Republic of Congo
ARQ Research Project and design proposal 2017

Panzi Hospital is an internationally recognized institution headed by the human-rights defender and Nobel Peace Prize winner Dr Denis Mukwege. The hospital was founded in 1999 in response to armed conflict within the DRC's eastern provinces. The region has been devastated by war and an epidemic of sexual violence that has had a huge impact on the lives of women and society as a whole. The EU Commission and several global aid organizations, including the Panzi Foundation in the United States, support Dr Mukwege in his mission to end violence against women and girls.

The healthcare model within the hospital is holistic and meets the entire range of patient needs: physical recovery, psychosocial and emotional support, community rehabilitation and legal aid. For the expansion of the mother and child unit, White undertook a corporate social responsibility project with Panzi Hospital, the Centre for Healthcare Architecture at Chalmers University, WSP Architects, the University of Gothenburg and Art of Life and Birth. During the first stages of design, it was agreed to conduct a feasibility study with a view to future-proofing the entire hospital site, improving safety and making sure that only resilient structures were added.

Within the brief to produce a health-promoting design, White focused in particular on making it sustainable and exploring how the building could be designed with the smallest possible carbon footprint. Other parts of our remit were to improve the site plan to solve logistical problems, update technical infrastructure, improve water and energy supplies, provide earthquake-proofing, manage flood risk within the hospital grounds and undertake long-term planning for the site to meet future needs. However, social considerations were always at the core of the project, the ambition being to build a new mother-and-child

unit that would be a model for modern maternity and neonatal care in central Africa.

Around 300 women give birth at Panzi Hospital every month, and the importance of building a safer and more efficient unit becomes clear when looking at survival rates in Kivu province. The infant mortality rate is 205 deaths per 1,000 births, and maternal mortality is 12 deaths per 1,000 births. (The figures for Sweden, by comparison, are 6 and 0.001 respectively.) Panzi Hospital focuses on meeting the UN Millennium Development Goals, which stipulate that maternal mortality should be reduced all over the world by 75 per cent.

Panzi Hospital was originally planned to hold 110 beds, focusing mainly on prenatal care and childbirth. However, in order to treat the many women suffering from delivery injuries and the large numbers affected by sexual violence, the hospital today has 450 beds. The existing maternal and neonatal care unit accommodates between 3,000 and 3,500 births per year.

The new unit needs a much-increased capacity, but that must be achieved in the most sustainable way possible. Since access to water and electricity is intermittent, comfort will be achieved through a bioclimatic design: the roof will be clad with solar panels to provide electricity; it will incorporate a system for rainwater collection; windows will optimize daylight, but shades and shutters will regulate it and help to reduce noise; strategically placed apertures will allow natural ventilation; and materials with high thermal mass will regulate the indoor temperature. The new birth rooms will fulfil the need for privacy, and new family visitor rooms will resolve the overcrowding that has long been a feature of the postnatal ward. There's little doubt that the new unit will be a source of pride and inspiration.

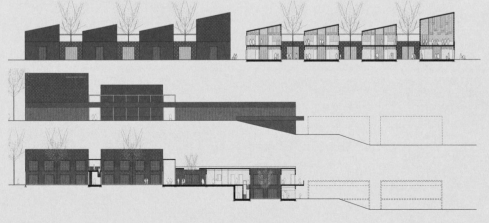

The new addition (in white) is designed to be easily navigable, prioritizing daylight, privacy and views out to nature to support the healing process. Each unit has private access to green courtyards for rehabilitation, recreation and social activities. Buildings are reached from a large entrance square via internal pathways.

← Sections of the hospital's simple modular buildings, which have been designed for minimal upkeep, as well as to withstand earthquakes. The roof's bioclimatic design plays a key role in optimizing electricity and water supply; natural ventilation is achieved by penetrated double walls, creating an electricity-free air-conditioning effect.

New Karolinska Solna

Solna, Sweden
Completed 2017

The New Karolinska Solna project is one of Sweden's largest-ever hospital projects and a crucial investment in developing a world-leading organization within life sciences. The immensity of the project, both as process and result, demanded new methods and collaborative strategies in almost every aspect, and made major use of building information modelling, in order to coordinate the huge volume of data passing between consultants, from visualization to detailed design and information management.

The new hospital building is designed to have minimal environmental impact, and is certified to LEED Gold standard. In fact, its energy consumption for electricity, heating and cooling is less than half that of most hospitals. Delivered through a combination of district heating, remote cooling and a separate geothermal plant, plus recycled energy from ventilation air, 99.7 per cent of its energy comes from renewable sources that have low CO_2 emissions. The hospital is a handsome and imposing presence in its urban location. A new subway station will be embedded into the entrance hall, thus integrating the hospital into the fabric of the city and its transport infrastructure.

More than a decade of evidence-based research into healthcare innovation, healing environments and the positive impact of architectural design – daylight, natural materials, views and more – has culminated in a building that focuses wholly on the well-being and recovery of the patients. For example, it incorporates as much daylight as possible, and vistas over the surroundings have been provided at every opportunity. Each ward contains 28 private patient rooms, all of which are flooded with natural light. Support functions, such as administrative offices, staff and conference rooms, are also orientated to receive maximum daylight. The public circulation space and lift access are housed in a glazed link between buildings, framing city and parkland views.

One of the principal aims of this project was to enhance the interaction between care, research and education while also focusing on sustainable and flexible use, and providing security and comfort for the patients. This is reflected in the architecture. The compact structure ensures the proximity of different functions, encouraging interdisciplinary working. The lower floors contain treatment rooms, X-ray and hospital services, while wards for 730 patients are on the upper levels. The entire project is designed and planned according to the guiding ethos 'patient first'. Each patient room measures ca18 square metres and is designed for single occupancy, thus enhancing privacy, confidence and medical security. All the rooms have their own en-suite bathroom and an additional bed to accommodate an overnight guest, as the support and close proximity of friends and family are crucial to recovery. Vital technical access points are integrated

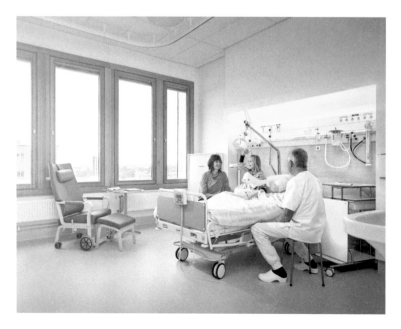

← Rooms are designed to be attractive and welcoming, so they have large windows to maximize natural light and views of the outside world. Technical access points are integrated into a panel above the bed, which keeps them accessible to staff but generally out of sight of the patient.

→ The hospital focuses on highly specialized healthcare and the state-of-the-art facilities inspire confidence in both patients and staff.

Overleaf: The New Karolinska Solna project is an urban hospital, which is part of the fabric of the city and a positive contribution to the neighbourhood.

into the bed-head panel to reduce the dominance of medical equipment, and advanced mobile medical equipment is stored in support zones on the ward. Strategically placed hand-washing stations and private hygiene rooms, plus smart logistical solutions, help to prevent the spread of infections.

The healthcare architecture has been developed in unison with groundbreaking clinical methods. Specialist clinicians, who have traditionally worked in separate clinics, are now part of thematic diagnostic care and treatment units. Support functions and equipment are inside the ward, close to small, decentralized nursing stations. Supplies can be quickly and efficiently moved around the building to and from the bedside, using pneumatic tubes and automated guided vehicles, which have their own dedicated lifts. These efficiencies avoid the need for patients to be wheeled long distances around the hospital to different diagnostic departments; instead, clinical teams take their equipment and expertise to the patient. The result is that medical staff are able to maximize their time with patients, and this in turn increases the confidence and well-being of the patients. Natural, tactile materials have been applied throughout the design; pale stone in the entrance plaza, light blonde ash wood for wall panelling and furniture, durable granite floors and white concrete elements all serve to lift and lighten the atmosphere. Colour and material palettes work thematically with the signage, lighting and public artworks to help people find their way around. Art plays an important therapeutic role in the hospital, enhancing the surroundings and benefiting patients, staff and visitors alike. In fact, the New Karolinska Solna project has received one of the most significant public art investments in Swedish history, and along with paintings, sculpture and mixed-media acquisitions, a number of site-specific artworks have been specially commissioned. The result is a civic building in which people can take pride.

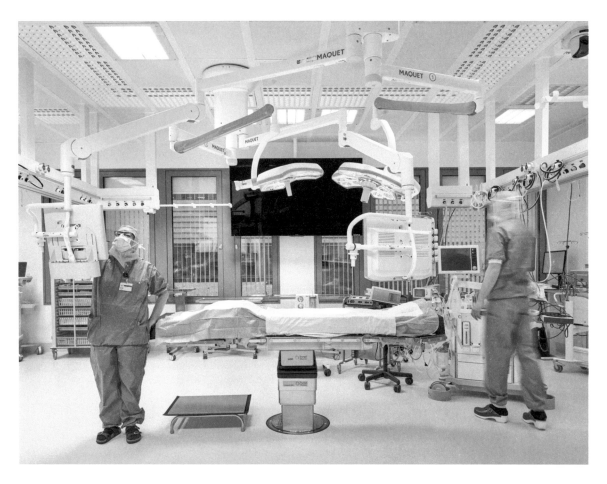

← The artworks (shown here are suspended glass objects by Fredrika Linder) interact with the architecture both inside and out, and are an important element in creating a good care environment.

↑ The exterior of the New Karolinska Solna project is streamlined and simple. Generous windows maximize the daylight that enters the building.

→ Seating is positioned in the communication areas, where wood and stone create a warm atmosphere.

Overleaf: The hospital is as much a new public space as a state-of-the-art healthcare facility. The openness and warmth of natural materials create a welcoming atmosphere for patients, relatives and staff. The 11-metre tall wall painting at the centre is by Andreas Eriksson.

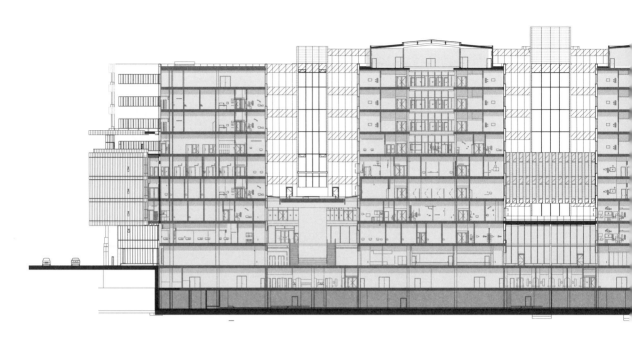

↑ The buildings at the eastern end of the hospital (in pink above) are wards, adapted to accommodate 24/7 activity, while the western ones (in green) operate more conventional working hours.

↓ → The drawing below and the aerial view on the right show how the hospital units connect to clinical research buildings and other academic institutions as one large campus.

Overleaf: Support functions and equipment are located discreetly within each ward, close to decentralized nursing stations. This means that equipment and diagnostic teams go to the patients, rather than the other way round.

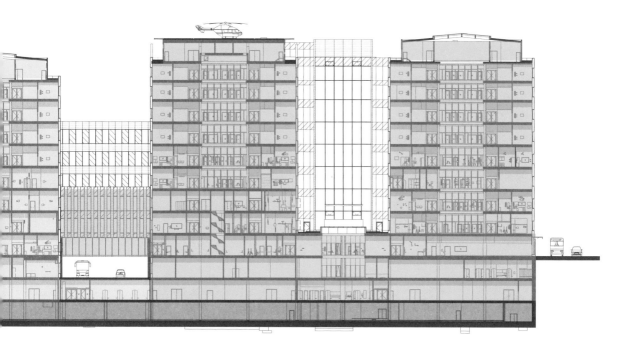

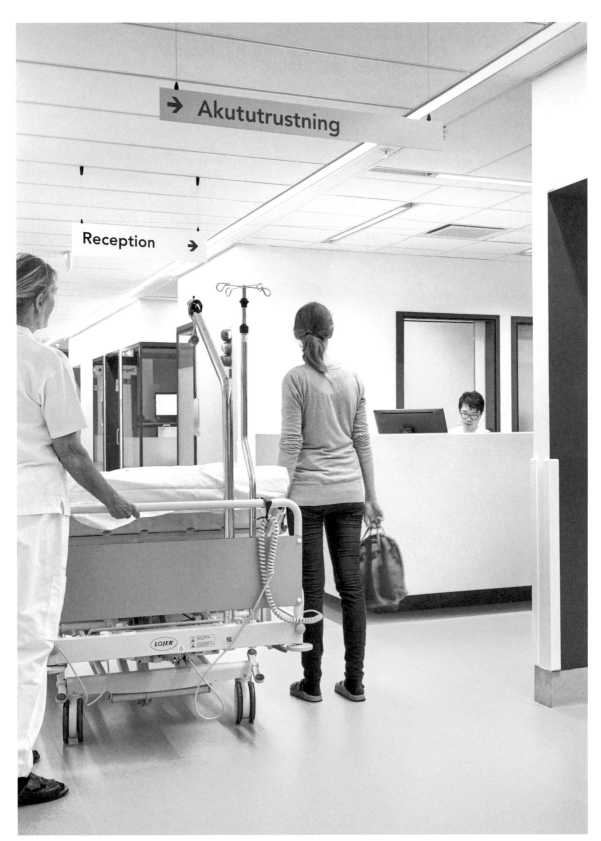

Hygienic Handle:
Reducing bacterial transfer by design

White Research Lab 2014

In a hospital environment, hand contamination is a constant problem, so reducing bacterial transfer is a crucial and continuous endeavour. Every surface touched by hands is a risk zone for transfer, and door handles are particularly exposed. The design of New Karolinska Solna is governed by the different hygiene compliances of the various spaces in the hospital. Swing doors are acceptable in most instances, but in some places fire regulations demand that doors open and shut by handle. As there was a gap in the market for door-opening solutions that fulfilled the high standards of contemporary hospital environments, Jörgen Pell, engineer at White, carried out a research project, which eventually became a new product called the Hygienic Handle. It is operated by pressing with the forearm and is thus able to radically reduce bacterial hand contamination.

In recent years, infections caused by drug-resistant bacteria have increased dramatically in all parts of the world. Indeed, anti-microbial resistance is a serious threat to global public health, and significantly increases the cost of healthcare. By helping staff and patients to avoid hand contact with door handles, a potential risk zone for bacterial transfer is eliminated.

An initial specification of demands, which arose from research and consultation with staff, resulted in White producing a 3D-printed prototype of the Hygienic Handle, and this was evaluated by the client and users. The design proposal passed the tests for manoeuvring with the forearm, and was also approved by fire regulations and accessibility standards. Pell then initiated a collaboration with the manufacturer Assa Abloy, and eventually the handle was incorporated into its product range. Following successful material tests, the Hygienic Handle could be installed in the hospital environment.

The anti-bacterial door handle is an innovative design that came about in direct response to the high standards of the New Karolinska University Hospital Solna project.

Carlanderska Hospital

Gothenburg, Sweden
Completed 2017

Carlanderska Hospital has provided specialist healthcare to public and private patients since 1927. The extension was added with great respect for Carlanderska's atmosphere and expression, to harmonize with the existing environment. The red-brick façade and copper roof unify the new and the old. The original buildings feature characteristic roofs, carefully finished with window dormers with various designs and frontispieces.

Several new large dormers on the ventilation room exterior intersect with the gutter and fit in line with the building's windows. The result is a 'jumping' gutter that constitutes the most characteristic feature of the building. The dormers serve several purposes: one holds the elevator equipment, while others provide possible opportunities for future changes to the building. All dormers are fitted with slanted glass lamellae in their façades, both to reflect light and to provide continuity in design.

The 7,000-square-metre extension, distributed over four floors and a basement, almost doubles the hospital area. The extension contains technology-intensive functions including seven surgery rooms, X-ray and sterilization rooms, as well as new entrances, staff facilities and a restaurant.

Between the new and old structures, a *hortus conclusus* – a walled garden – reminiscent of an organized and sectioned monastery garden, functions as an outdoor waiting room. Despite the extension's significant volume, the park remains largely intact and the walkways retain their original paths. The care-giving facility has retained its charm throughout the modifications to its original state, thanks to a deep respect for the living heritage of the hospital grounds.

↓ The courtyard is inspired by medieval monastery gardens, dissected by walkways and planted with aromatic herbs and flowers.

→ The brick façade is laid with great respect to the craft and tradition invested in the original buildings. The walkway is a well-needed addition to interior logistics, and offers a view of the garden.

↘ With their calm and soothing appearance, the well-lit interiors are easy to navigate.

Project Facts

INTRODUCTION
Make Sense exhibition
Location: Architekturgalerie München, Germany
Status: Completed 2017
Lead architect: Max Zinnecker
Team: Rickard Andersson, Sebastian Muehlbauer,
Peter Nilsson, Margaret Steiner, Malin Zimm
Gallery owner: Nicola Borgmann, Architekturgalerie München

LIVE AND LET LIVE
Koggens Gränd
Location: Malmö, Sweden
Status: Completed 2012
Client: White Arkitekter AB
Lead architect: Maud Karlström
Team: Milad Barosen, Bernt Borgestig, Daniel Borrie, Niels de Bruin,
Andreas Frykman, Anna Graaf, Maud Karlström, Mattias Lind, Nadja
Lindhe, Jenny Nordius Stålhamre, James Reader, Rebecka Wijk.
Environmental certification: Miljöbyggnad Guld (Environmental
Design Level Gold)
Awards: Sweden Green Building Awards 2014 (nomination)

Frodeparken
Location: Uppsala, Sweden
Status: Completed 2013
Client: Uppsalahem AB
Lead architect: Mats Egelius
Team: Mats Egelius, Hanna Linde, Marja Lundgren, Jens Modin,
Mattias Nordström, Oskar Norelius, Anders Olausson, Stefan Rummel,
Charlotta Wallander, Henrik Wallander
Environmental certification: Svanen
Awards: Solar Energy Award (Solenergipriset) honourable mention
2015, Green Future Award 2014 (Skanska Gröna Framtidspris)

MultiBO: A new model for student living
Researcher: Kristoffer Roxbergh, White Research Lab 2016
Status: Concept design 2015
Concept architect: Kristoffer Roxbergh
Team: Katharina Björlin Wiklund, Anders Bobert, Dan Engberg, Karolina
Nyström, Kristoffer Roxbergh
Report title: Framtidens studentbostäder
Report co-authored by: White Arkitekter, Studentbostadsföretagen
(Swedish non-profit governing student housing standards), Stockholms
studentbostäder (the Stockholm Student Housing Foundation)

Kvarteret Båtsman
Location: Stockholm, Sweden
Status: Completed 2012
Client: Besqab
Lead architect: Mats Egelius
Team: Mats Egelius, Gunnar Hidemark, Zlatko Pilipovic,
Charlotta Wallander

Climate Innovation District
Location: Leeds, United Kingdom
Status: Concept design 2016
Client: Citu
Lead architect: Geoff Denton
Team: Geoff Denton, Linda Thiel

Äppelträdgården
Location: Gothenburg, Sweden
Status: Completed 2011
Client: KB Skolmössan – FO Peterson & Söner Byggnads AB & White
Arkitekter AB
Lead architect: Thomas Landenberg

Team: Helena Bjarnegård, Sam Keshavarz, Thomas Landenberg, Mikael
Stenqvist, Christian Wahlström, Lars Zackrisson
Environmental certification: Miljöbyggnad Guld (Environmental
Design Level Gold)
Awards: Bostadspriset 2011

Eyes of Runavík
Location: Runavík, Faroe Islands
Status: Competition proposal 2016
Client: Nordic Built Cities
Lead architect: Mikkel Thams Olsen
Team: Brooke Campbell-Johnston, Iben Degn Pedersen, Charlotte
Falstrup, Rickard Nygren, Viktor Sjöberg, Mikkel Thams Olsen
Environmental certification: Awards: Nordic Built Cities
Challenge 2016

Future Recycling Centre
Location: Stockholm, Sweden
Researcher: Lise-Lott Larsson Kolessar, White Research Lab 2016
Status: Completed 2015
Lead architect: Tomas Landefeldt
Team: Jenni Brink Bylund, Tomas Landfeldt,
Lise-Lott Larsson Kolessar
Client: The City of Stockholm, Stockholm Vatten
Responsible specialist: Lise-Lott Larsson Kolessar

Friggagatan
Location: Gothenburg, Sweden
Status: Completed 2011
Client: Stigberget
Lead architect: Jan Larsson
Team: Martin Clase, John Johansson, Jan Larsson, Måns Larsson,
Kristina Ohlsson, Mikael Stenqvist, Lars Zackrisson

Dream Home
Researcher: Barbara Vogt, White Research Lab 2016
Location: Linköping, Sweden
Status: Completed 2017
Client: Stångåstaden
Lead architect: Ingrid Ehrnebo
Team: Ingrid Ehrnebo, Susanne Klämfeldt, Cuong Ly, Barbara Vogt

Kvarteret Ankaret
Location: Alingsås, Sweden
Status: Completed 2016
Client: Handelshus i Alingsås AB, Skanska Sverige AB
Lead architect: Thomas Landenberg
Team: Johanna Bocian Östberg, Jessica Kos, Thomas Landenberg,
Bruno Manrique Carrera, Sofia Tillberg, Christian Wahlström,
Cecilia Wretlind

Lilla Tellus Masterplan
Location: Stockholm, Sweden
Status: Concept design 2016
Client: Alm Equity, Scanprop Development AB
Lead architect: Oskar Norelius
Team: Jonatan Ahlmark, Malin Alenius, David Alton, Milad Barosen,
Elena Bloch, Mike Fedak, Monika Hellekant, Jacob Högberg, Johan
Holkers, Jack Johnson, Raimo Joss, Sam Keshavarz, Koen Kragting,
Viktor Nilsson, Oskar Norelius, Pontus Pyk, Mats Selin, Lukas Thiel,
Thomas Zaar

A Century of Daylight: Natural light in residential architecture
Researchers: Malin Alenius, Marja Lundgren, White Research Lab 2015
Status: Exhibition and publication Bo.Nu.Då at ArkDes (Swedish Centre
for Architecture and Design) 2015–16

Slussplan
Location: Malmö, Sweden
Status: Completed 2014
Client: JM AB
Lead architect: Sven Gustafsson
Team: Maria Ekenberg, Sven Gustafsson, Maud Karlström, Markus Magnusson, Martin Vozzi
Awards: Urban Design Awards Malmö: residential building category 2014

Vävskedsgatan
Location: Gothenburg, Sweden
Status: Completed 2005
Client: KB Lunden (White Arkitekter and FO Peterson & Söner)
Lead architect: Johan Lundin
Team: Joakim Hansson, Kurt Hedberg, Dan Larsson, Nadja Lindhe, Johan Lundin, Thomas Samuelsson, Simon Svensson
Awards: Kasper Salin Prize 2006 (nomination), Stora samhällsbyggarpriset 2005 (nomination), Best Building Gothenburg 2005, Årets Bygge 2005

TRANSFORM THE PUBLIC
Kiruna Masterplan
Location: Kiruna, Sweden
Status: New urban development plan 2013
Client: Kiruna municipality
Lead architects: Krister Lindstedt, Mikael Stenqvist, Sam Keshavarz
Team: Martin Bergqvist, Åsa Bjerndell, Christoph Duckart, Anna Edblom, Peter Eklund, Jack Johnson, Martin Johnson, Sam Keshavarz, Koen Kragting, Krister Lindstedt, Mikael Stenqvist, Ivar Suneson
Sustainability experts: Åsa Keane, Viktoria Walldin, Jan Wijkmark
Consultants: Ghilardi + Hellsten arkitekter, Spacescape, Tyréns, TX Trivector, Sweco

White Public: The role of the architect in public building
Researcher: Erik Torvén, White Research Lab 2014
Report title: White Public – arkitektur och politik
Status: White Research Lab research report 2015
In collaboration with: Karin Stenqvist and Viktoria Walldin (White Arkitekter), Jesper Meijling and Helena Mattsson (KTH)

Bee Connected
Location: Gothenburg, Sweden
Status: Completed 2016
Client: Chalmers University of Technology
In collaboration with: Chalmers School of Architecture, Mareld Landskapsarkitekter
Responsible architect: Linda Ekman
Team: Ulrika Bergbrant, Linda Ekman, Oskar Ivarsson, Martin Allik (Mareld Landskapsarkitekter), Meta Berghauser Pont (Chalmers)

Green Space Factor
Researchers: Felicia Sjösten Harlin, Jan Wijkmark, ARQ research project 2016
Report title: Grönytefaktor för allmän platsmark 2.0 (GYF AP)
Client: C/O city – Urbana ekosystemtjänster
Status: Report published in 2016, 2018
Team: Felicia Sjösten Harlin, Jan Wijkmark, Malin Romo (White), Emmelie Nilsson (Stockholms stad), Helena Jeppsson, Marie Åslund, Felix Brännlund, Martin Rask (WSP)
In collaboration with: Christina Wikberger (Stockholms stad)

Brovaktarparken
Concept: (nod) C-O-M-B-I-N-E
Executive architect: White Arkitekter
Location: Stockholm, Sweden

Status: Completed 2013
Client: The City of Stockholm
Lead architect: Sofia Waernulf
Team: Angelica Bierfelt Liptak, Jenny Mathiasson, Jonas Runberger, Sofia Waernulf
Awards: Sienapriset 2014 (Swedish Landscape Architecture Award)

Chameleon Cabin
Location: Mobile structure, Tjolöholm Castle, Sweden
Status: Completed 2013
Lead architect: Mattias Lind
Client: Göteborgstryckeriet

Girls' Room in Public Space
Researchers: Moa Lindunger, Rebecca Rubin, Anna Ågren, Angelica Åkerman, White Research Lab 2015
Report title: Flickrum i det offentliga
Status: Lectures, workshops, seminars, debates and more, 2016–17
In collaboration with: teenage girls from Skarpnäck municipality, pedagogues from Skarpnäck municipality, theatre group UngaTur, Skarpnäcks ungdomsråd

Pallis Pop-up Park
Location: Stockholm, Sweden
Status: Completed 2015
In collaboration with: Fastighetsägarna (Pallis)
Responsible architects: Erik Kiltorp, Kristina Philipson

St Johannesplan
Location: Malmö, Sweden
Status: Completed 2011
Client: The City of Malmö, Church of Sweden
Lead architect: Niels de Bruin
Team: Niels de Bruin, Anna Eklund, Gustav Jarlöv, Andreas Milsta
In collaboration with: Ebba Matz (artist)

Bäckparken
Location: Linköping, Sweden
Status: Completed 2016
Client: Linköping municipality
Lead architect: Linda Moström
Team: Charlotta Davidsson, Johan Kauppi, Linda Moström, Mikael Norman, Barbara Vogt

Kungsbacka Torg
Location: Kungsbacka, Sweden
Status: Completed 2012
Client: Kungsbacka municipality
Lead architects: Sam Keshavarz, Paula Mackenzie
Team: Mikaela Åström Forsgren, Ulla Antonsson, Sam Keshavarz, Paula Mackenzie

Södra Skanstull Masterplan
Location: Skanstull, Stockholm, Sweden
Status: Masterplan 2017
Client: The City of Stockholm (Exploateringskontoret och Stadsbyggnadskontoret)
Lead architect: Krister Lindstedt
Team: Anna Ågren, Jens Andersson, Elin Henriksson, Krister Lindstedt, Martin Login, Oskar Nordqvist, Hanna Plato, Rebecca Rubin, Ulrika Stenkula, Ivar Suneson
In collaboration with: AJ-Landskap, WSP-group, Spacescape, Anna Birath (Nyréns)
Awards: Planpriset 2017 Sveriges Arkitekter, WAFX Prize: Ageing and health category

Stadsberget
Location: Piteå, Sweden
Status: Completed 2015
Client: Piteå municipality
Lead architect: Lennart Sjögren

The Forumtorget Bench
Location: Uppsala, Sweden
Status: Completed 2018
Client: Uppsala municipality
Responsible architect: Gustav Jarlöv
Team: Hamia Aghaiemeybodi, Torbjörn Eliasson, Gustav Jarlöv,
Sam Keshawarz, Hanna Linde, Lotta Lindh, Jens Modin,
Vladimir Ondejcik, Jonas Runberger, Pedram Seddighsadeh,
Theodor Tsesmatzoglou, Viktoria Walldin
In collaboration with: Konsthuset Uppsala, LYX, Jonas Wannfors,
DesigntoProduction, Rosskopf + Partners

Tele2 Arena
Location: Stockholm, Sweden
Status: Completed 2013
Client: Stockholm Globe Arenas SGA
Lead architects: Fredrik Källström, Monica von Schmalensee
Team: Mats Anslöv, Anders Bobert, Lejla Cengic, Magnus Croon,
Martin Edfelt, Erik Eriksson, Eva Fabricius, Magdalena Franciskovic, Elin
Hammarsten, Jens Hansson, Rosmari Johansson, Raimo Joss, Jesper
Källgren, Fredrik Källström, Bengt Mührer, Robert Niziolek,
Dirk Noack, Björn Norén, Nadja Odenhage, Thomas Rudin, Monica von
Schmalensee, Björn Tegnell, Hampus Trotzig, Sofia Waernulf, Joacim
Wahlström
Environmental certification: Miljöbyggnad Guld (Environmental Design
Level Gold)
Awards: Arena of the Year 2014

Heden Exercise Park
Location: Gothenburg, Sweden
Status: Completed 2014
Client: White as consultant to ÅF AB for The City of Gothenburg
Lead architect: Lena Osvalds
Team: Mikaela Åström Forsgren, Joel Hördin, Anika Meinche, Lena
Osvalds

MEET, LEARN AND CREATE
Väven Cultural Centre
Location: Umeå, Sweden
Status: Completed 2014
Client: Umeå municipality, Balticgruppen
Architects: White Arkitekter and Snøhetta
Executive architect: White Arkitekter
Lead architects: Maria Olsson, Lennart Sjögren
Team: Jan Anundi, Katharina Björlin Wiklund, Maeva Chardon, Anna-
Carin Dahlberg, August Edwards, Pernilla Engberg, Malin Ericson, Anna
von Gegerfelt, Åsa Haremst, Mats Holmberg, Albin Holmgren, Johanna
Larsson, Maria Olsson, Nilda Pulga, Katarina Rasmusson, Agne Revellé,
Marianne Rutberg, Lennart Sjögren, Marie-France Stendahl, Gunnar
Stomrud, Mirja Westling, Jonas Westman
In collaboration with: Tyréns, Sweco system, Ramböll, AIX arkitekter,
ÅF lighting
Environmental certification: Miljöbyggnad silver
(Environmental Design Level Silver): certification pending
Awards: Kasper Salin Award 2014

Bråtejordet Secondary School
Location: Strømmen, Norway
Status: Completed 2014
Client: Skedsmo municipality

Lead architect: Thomas Landenberg
Team: Karin Jakobsson, Thomas Landenberg, Karin Sjödin,
Christian Wahlström, Lars Zackrisson
In collaboration with: Norconsult
Environmental certification: Norwegian Energiklasse B

Dynamic Daylight in Schools
Researcher: Mikaela Åström Forsgren, White Research Lab 2014
Report title: Dynamiskt ljus – Fokus Skola
In collaboration with: Philips, Fagerhult

Skellefteå Cultural Centre
Location: Skellefteå, Sweden
Status: Competition proposal 2017
Client: Skellefteå municipality
Lead architects: Oskar Norelius, Robert Schmitz
Team: Katharina Björlin Wiklund, Marta Bohlmark, Axel Bodros
Wolgers, Patrik Buchinger, Magnus Croon, Sarah Dahman Meyersson,
Amanda Ersson, Charles Gårdeman, Jens Hansson, Anders Johnsson,
Jesper Källgren, Fredrik Källström, Maria Laakso, Robert Niziolek, Marte
Noedtvedt Skjaeggestad, Oskar Norelius, Björn Norén, Maria Orvesten,
Marianne Rutberg, Robert Schmitz, Mats Sehlin, Gustav Söderberg
Röstlund, Pernilla Svedberg, Björn Vestlund, Ulrika Wallin
In collaboration with: Dipl. Ing. Florian Kosche AS, INCOORD,
Brandskyddslaget, ACAD, Karl Tyrväinen

Færder Technical College
Location: Tønsberg, Norway
Status: Completed 2014
Client: SKUP (School Development Project) Tønsberg, Vestfold
Fylkeskommune
Lead architect: Karin Björning-Engström
Team: Karin Björning-Engström, Björn Bondesson, Karin Jakobsson,
Sam Keshavarz, Thomas Landenberg, Paula Mackenzie, Carl Molin,
Roger Olsson, Peter Ylmén

Bildmuseet
Location: Umeå, Sweden
Status: Completed 2012
Client: Balticgruppen Design AB
Architects: White Arkitekter in collaboration with Henning Larsen
Lead architect: Lennart Sjögren
Team: Olov Bergström, Gustav Jarlöv, Marianne Rutberg,
Lennart Sjögren
Awards: Mies van der Rohe Award 2013 (nomination)

Selma Community Centre
Location: Gothenburg, Sweden
Status: Concept design 2017
Client: Göteborgslokaler, The City of Gothenburg
Lead architect: Mattias Lind
Team: Karin Heden, Theresa Kjellberg, Jessica Kos, Mattias Lind, Sofia
Lundberg, Jacob Lundqvist, Samuel Michaëlsson, Jacob Nilsson, Linn
Roldin, Daniel Stenqvist, Christian Wahlström, Britta Wikholm, Lars
Zackrisson

The GoDown Arts Centre in Nairobi: Building for a young
democracy
Researcher: Ulrika Stenkula, ARQ research project 2015
Client/partner: The GoDown Arts Centre
Location: Nairobi, Kenya
Status: Feasibility study 2015–16
Report title: The GoDown Arts Centre

The GoDown Arts Centre
Location: Nairobi, Kenya
Status: Concept design 2014
Client/partner: The GoDown Arts Centre
Lead architect: Ulrika Stenkula
Team: Marta Bohlmark, Erik Kiltorp, Dirk Noack, Ulrika Stenkula,
Filip Sudolsky, Viktoria Walldin, Ulrika Wallin
In collaboration with: The GoDown Arts Centre, Planning Systems Ltd

Messingen
Location: Upplands Väsby, Sweden
Status: Completed 2011
Client: Upplands Väsby municipality, Peab
Lead architects: Hans Forsmark, Klara Frosterud
Team: Maja Abrahamson, Pelle Beckman, Katharina Björlin Wiklund,
Martin Ceder, Anders Danielsson, Martin Edfelt, Erik Eriksson, Sofia
Eskilsdotter, Hans Forsmark, Magdalena Franciskovic, Klara Frosterud,
Yara Hormazábal Cortés, Marie Hult, Karin Höök, Leif Johansson,
Rosmari Johansson, Raimo Joss, Elise Juusela-Norberg, Lovisa
Kihlborg, Petter Lindencrona, Kåre Lundberg, Frida Munktell, Jonas
Nilsson, Margaretha Nilsson, Robert Niziolek, Frida Nordström, Björn
Norén, Karolina Nyström, Martin Öhman, Anders Olausson, Marie
Oldfeldt, Sofia Palmer, Kajsa Paulsson, Björn Rubin, Amelie Rydqvist,
Niklas Singstedt, Hans Swensson, Anders Thalberg, Anna Ulrichs,
Kaveh Vaez, Mats Wåhlin, Viktoria Walldin, Anders Wiil, Jan Wijkmark,
Per Wikfeldt
Awards: Stora Samhällsbyggnadspriset 2012

The Humanities Theatre
Location: Uppsala, Sweden
Status: Completed 2017
Client: Akademiska Hus Uppsala
Lead architects: Jacob Melin, Nina Wittlöv Löfving
Team: Sven Gunnarson, Stefan Johansson, Frans Magnusson,
Jacob Melin, Daban Mohammed Ali, Lina Nilsson, Annika Reizenstein,
Vladimir Ondejcik, Jonas Runberger, Solveig Sennerholm, Pia Wacker,
Anders Wiil, Nina Wittlöv Löfving
In collaboration with: Ann Lislegaard (artist)
Environmental certification: Miljöbyggnad Silver (Environmental Design
Level Silver)
Awards: Plåtpriset 2018 (Swedish prize for sheet-metal architecture),
Aluminiumpriset 2018 (Swedish Design Awards), Årets Bygge 2018
(Building of the Year)

Billingskolan
Location: Skövde, Sweden
Status: Completed 2014
Client: Skövde municipality
Lead architect: Karin Björning-Engström
Team: Karin Björning-Engström, Björn Bondesson,
Karin Jakobsson, Nadja Lindhe, Jeroen Matthijssen, Elisabeth
Rosenlund, Rikard Sjöberg, Karin Sjödin, Katharina Thullner
Environmental certification: Miljöbyggnad Guld (Environmental
Design Level Gold)

The Street of Lights
Researcher and team leader: Christina Vildinge, White Research
Lab 2016, Business & DesignLab, Göteborgs universitet
Team: Hannah Griffiths (GöteborgsOperan), Andreas Milsta,
Christina Vildinge (White Arkitekter), Mathias Strömer (Swedish
Exhibition Agency), Lina Ikse, Pecka Söderberg (Konstepidemin)
In collaboration with: The local council, SDF East Göteborg and
Cultural Affairs Administration
Location: Gothenburg, Sweden
Status: Temporary installation 2016–17
Report title: Design as driver of learning and innovation
Awards: Gothenburg City Intercultural Award

The Public Light Lab
Researcher and team leader: Christina Vildinge, White Research
Lab 2016, ARQ research project 2015, Business & DesignLab,
Göteborgs universitet
Location: Gothenburg, Sweden
Status: Temporary structure 2016
Team: Joel Björberg, Pereric Dahlberg, Hannah Griffiths
(GöteborgsOperan), Jesper Cederlund, Gustav Löfgren, Mathias
Strömer (Swedish Exhibition Agency), Andreas Milsta, Kajsa Sperling,
Christina Vildinge (White Arkitekter)
In collaboration with: The local council, SDF East Göteborg,
Cultural Affairs Administration and Konstepidemin Arts and
Culture Centre
Report title: Design for social innovation
Awards: Göteborg Energi

Cirkus Skandiascenen
Location: Stockholm, Sweden
Status: Completed 2015
Client: Förvaltningsbolaget Cirkus, NCC Construction (client in
construction document stage)
Lead architect: Anders Arfvidsson
Team: Anders Arfvidsson, Patric Buchinger, Jens Hansson,
Tove Jägerhök, Camilla Kappel
Awards: Glaspriset 2016 (nomination), Årets Stockholmsbyggnad 2016
(nomination, Building of the year awards),
Svenska Fönster-priset 2016 (nomination)

LET NATURE LEAD
Naturum Kosterhavet
Location: Koster, Sweden
Status: Completed 2012
Client: Naturvårdsverket (The Swedish Environmental Protection
Agency), The County Administrative Board of Västra Götaland
Lead architects: Ulla Antonsson, Mattias Lind
Team: Anders Åkeflo, Pär Andréasson, Ulla Antonsson, Magnus Bunner,
Anna Graaf, Andreas Laessker, Mattias Lind, Magnus Nellström,
Mathias Nilsson, Agne Revellé, Kairn Sjödin
Environmental certification: Miljöbyggnad Guld (Environmental
Design Level Gold)
Awards: Kasper Salin Award 2013 (nomination),
Helge Zimdal Award 2013 (nomination)

Hasle Harbour Baths
Location: Bornholm, Denmark
Status: Completed 2013
Client: Bornholm regional municipality
Lead architect: Fredrik Pettersson
Team: Katrine Hvidt, Martin Münter, Fredrik Pettersson,
Martin Sundberg, Mikkel Thams Olsen

Birdwatchers' Sheaf Shack
Location: Toronto, Canada
Status: Competition proposal 2016
Client: Winter Stations, Toronto
Lead architect: Niels de Bruin
Team: Niels de Bruin, Hanna Johansson, Karolina Nilsson,
Vladimir Ondejcik, Jonas Runberger

Naturum Store Mosse
Location: Hillerstorp, Sweden
Status: Completed 2003
Client: The County Administrative Board of Jönköping,
Statens Fastighetsverk (The National Property Board of Sweden)
Lead architects: Ulla Antonsson, Mattias Lind
Team: Lisbeth Andersson, Ulla Antonsson, Daniel Hultman,

Mattias Lind, Roger Olsson, Lars Zackrisson
Awards: Träpriset 2008 (nomination)

Naturum Vänerskärgården Victoria House
Location: Lidköping, Sweden
Status: Completed 2013
Client: Statens Fastighetsverk (The National Property Board of Sweden)
Lead architect: Mattias Lind, Ulla Antonsson
Team: Pär Andreasson, Ulla Antonsson, Mattias Lind, Agne Revellé, Moa Wendt

Free-form Timber: From design to fabrication
Innochain and Dsearch/White Research Lab 2015
Researcher: Tom Svilans
Research project title: Integrated material practice in free-form timber structures
Project affiliation: CITA (Centre for IT and Architecture), KADK (Royal Danish Academy of Fine Arts, Schools of Architecture, Design and Conservation), Blumer-Lehmann AG, White Arkitekter
Status: Thesis work in progress, competition proposal 2017

The Royal Pavilion, Southend Pier
Location: Southend-on-Sea, United Kingdom
Status: Completed 2012
Client: Southend-on-Sea Borough Council
Lead architects: Fredrik Pettersson, Niels de Bruin
Team: Niels de Bruin, Katarina Hennig, Sam Keshavarz, Niels Majgaard, Mikkel Olsen, Fredrik Pettersson
Awards: World Architecture Festival Awards 2010 (nomination), Mipim Awards: Future Projects Landscape 2013 (nomination), RIBA East Regional Award for Best Refurbished Building 2013, Surface Design Award 2013

Karlshamn Bath House
Location: Karlshamn, Sweden
Status: Completed 2015
Client: Kallbadhusets vänner
Lead architect: Sven Gustafsson
Team: Emilie Dafgård, Ola Dellson, Sven Gustafsson
Environmental certification: Is there info missing?
Awards: Karlshamns Stadsbyggnadspris 2015 (Urban Planning Award)

Hamra National Park and Crown Jewels
Location: Ljusdal, Sweden
Status: Completed 2013
Client: The County Administrative Board of Gävleborg
Lead architect: Martin Ehn Hillberg
Team: Ulla Antonsson, Magnus Bunner, Martin Ehn Hillberg, Kerstin Lagnefeldt, Mattias Nordström, Agne Revellé, Anders Tväråna
[Crown Jewels:]
Clients: The County Administrative Board of Gävleborg, Naturvårdsverket (The Swedish Environmental Protection Agency)
Status: Completed 2011
Lead architects: Mattias Lind, Ulla Antonsson
Team: Ulla Antonsson, Magnus Bunner, Mattias Lind, Magnus Nellström, Mattias Nordström, Agne Revellé
Awards: Sienapriset 2013 (Swedish Landscape Architecture Award),

Naturum Vattenriket
Location: Kristianstad, Sweden
Status: Completed 2011
Client: Kristianstad municipality
Lead architect: Fredrik Pettersson
Team: Per-Anders Andersson, Per Berg, Ulrika Connheim, Anders Danielsson, Niels de Bruin, Jakob Ek, Johan Larsson, Fredrik Pettersson, Martin Sundberg

Naturum Oset
Location: Örebro, Sweden
Status: Completion planned 2019
Client: Örebroporten, Örebro municipality
Lead architects: Mattias Lind, Björn Bondesson, Martin Ehn Hillberg
Team: Björn Bondesson, Viktoria Buskqvist, Martin Ehn Hillberg, Mattias Lind, Hanna Linde, Rickard Nygren, Agne Revellé, Linn Roldin, Britta Wikholm, BDAB/Max Tillberg

Naturum Fulufjället
Location: Älvdalen, Sweden
Status: Completed 2003
Client: Naturvårdsverket (The Swedish Environmental Protection Agency)
Lead architect: Gunilla Hagberg
Team: Karin Ahlzén, Gunilla Hagberg, Mattias Nordström, Christer Uppfeldt
Awards: Träpriset 2004 (nomination)

Kastrup Sea Bath
Location: Tårnby, Denmark
Status: Completed 2005
Client: Tårnby municipality
Lead architect: Fredrik Pettersson
Team: Johnny Gere, Henrik Haremst, Fredrik Pettersson, Rasmus Skaarup, Pernille Vermund, Göran Wihl, NIRAS, Planlæggere A/S
Awards: Architectural Review Award for Emerging Architecture 2006 (honourable mention), Mies van der Rohe Award 2007 (nomination), Olympic Committee Bronze medal: sport and leisure building 2009

Amber Road Trekking Cabins
Location: Baltic Sea Coastline, Latvia
Status: Competition proposal 2017
Client: The BeeBreeders Amber Road Trekking Cabin competition
Lead architect: Scott Grbavac
Team: Andreea Cutieru, Santiago Carlos Peña Fiorda, Scott Grbavac

MAKE WORKPLACES THAT WORK
Johanneberg Science Park
Location: Gothenburg, Sweden
Status: Completed 2015
Client: Chalmers University, Johanneberg Science Park
Lead architects: Mattias Lind, Johan Lundin
Team: Elin Adolfsson, Egil Blom, Maria Glädt, Viktor Göthe, Karin Hedén, Joel Hördin, Andreas Laessker, Mattias Lind, Johan Lundin, Karin Lundin, Mathias Nilsson, Erik Nygren, Lars Zackrisson
Environmental certification: Miljöbyggnad Guld (Environmental Design Level Gold)

White's Stockholm Office
Location: Stockholm, Sweden
Status: Completed 2003
Client: White Arkitekter AB
Lead architect: Bengt Svensson
Team: Marie Hult, Kjell Jensfelt, Marja Lundgren, Jenny Mathiasson, Linda Mattsson, Mikael Sewon, Bengt Svensson, Per Wikfeldt, Åke Wilén
Environmental certification: Miljöbyggnad Guld (Environmental Design Level Gold)
Awards: Kasper Salin Award 2003, Svensk Betong Arkitekturpris 2004, Mies van der Rohe Award 2005 (nomination)

Façade Design for Optimized Daylighting
Researcher: Marja Lundgren, ARQ Research project 2013
Status: Competition proposal 2013, ARQ Research report 2014
Report title: Daylight autonomy and façade design: From research to

practice for the Stockholm SEB Bank head office
Research team/co-author: Marie-Claude Dubois

An Architecture Studio
Location: Kiruna, Sweden
Status: Completed 2015
Client: White Arkitekter AB
Lead architect: Martin Johnson
Team: Martin Johnson, Tomas Landfeldt

P5 Väven
Location: Umeå, Sweden
Status: Completed 2015
Client: Balticgruppen AB
Lead architect: Mattias Lind
Team: Mikaela Åström Forsgren, Egil Blom, Malgorzata Kosieradzka,
Annie Leonsson, Mattias Lind, Andreas Milsta, Andreas Ohlsson, Maria
Olsson, Agne Revellé, Marianne Rutberg, Lennart Sjögren, Christian
Wahlström

Oslo Government Centre
Location: Oslo, Norway
Status: Competition proposal 2015
Client: Statsbygg
Lead architect: Sara Grahn
Team: Ellen Aga Kildal, Sara Grahn, Jenny Mäki, Jeroen Mathijssen,
Alf Isak Nordli, Mattias Nordström, Viktoria Walldin
In collaboration with: Alliance arkitekter AS, Sweco Infrastruktur AB

Epidemic Sound
Location: Stockholm, Sweden
Status: Completed 2015
Client: Epidemic Sound
Lead architect: Karolina Nyström
Team: Mikaela Åström Forsgren, Märta Friman, Rebecca Edwards
Mannheimer, Karolina Nyström

Transformer Station
Location: Uppsala, Sweden
Status: Completed 2009
Client: Vattenfall
Lead architect: Christer Uppfeld
Team: Lars Höglund, Charlotta Råsmark, Christer Uppfeld

UR Educational Broadcasting Company
Location: Stockholm, Sweden
Status: Completed 2011
Client: UR, the Swedish Educational Broadcasting Company
Lead architects: Linda Thiel, Åsa Esseen Wiking, Märta Friman (interior
architecture)
Team: Magnus Croon, Åsa Esseen Wiking, Jake Ford,
Märta Friman, Tomas Landfeldt, Stefano Mangili, Anders Parment, Linda
Thiel, Kaveh Vaez, Sofia Waernulf

Quality Hotel Globen Event Hall
Location: Stockholm, Sweden
Status: Completed 2014
Client: Arcona, Choice Hotels
Lead architects: Magnus Croon, Sander Schuur
Team: Hamia Aghaiemeybodi, Magnus Croon, Hanna Plato,
Jonas Runberger, Sander Schuur, Pedram Seddigzadeh
Environmental certification: Miljöbyggnad Guld (Environmental
Design Level Gold)
In collaboration with: C&D Snickeri (producer)

Växjö City Hall and Central Station
Location: Växjö, Sweden
Status: Competition proposal 2016
Client: Vöfab, Växjö kommun, Jernhusen
Lead architect: Klara Frosterud
Team: Rafel Crespo Solana, Klara Frosterud, Åsa Haremst,
Sam Keshavarz, Koen Kragting, Mattias Nordström, Rickard Nygren,
Erik Torvén, Theodor Tsesmatzoglou
In collaboration with: Constructors DIFK AS: Florian Kosche and
Sandra Elbe

Täby Municipal Hall
Location: Täby, Sweden
Status: Completed 2017
Client: Täby municipality
Lead architects: Thomas Rudin, Robert Schmitz
Team: Milad Barosen, Angelica Bierfeldt Liptak, Johan Björkholm, Bernt
Borgestig, Amanda Ersson, Magdalena Franciskovic,
Fredric Kihlberg, Anton Kolbe, Tomas Landfeldt, Thomas Rudin, Robert
Schmitz
Environmental certification: Miljöbyggnad Guld (Environmental
Design Level Gold)
Awards: IDA International design award 2017

Swedish Energy Agency
Location: Eskilstuna, Sweden
Status: Completed 2017
Client: Energimyndigheten (Swedish Energy Agency)
Lead architect: Elin Rooth
Team: Maja Abrahamsson, Olle Gustafsson, Lisa Läckgren,
Nicole Morel, Elin Rooth
Visuals: Emil Fagander

The Hub
Location: Uppsala, Sweden
Status: Completed 2017
Client: Vasakronan
Lead architect: Anders Tväråna
Team: Aksel Alvarez Jurgueson, Young Ill Kim, Karin Leckström, Hedvig
Norberg, Ylva Reddy, Anna Röjdeby, Anders Tväråna

DESIGN FOR CARE AND HEALING
Aabenraa Psychiatric Hospital
Location: Aabenraa, Denmark
Status: Completed 2015
Client: Region Syddanmark
Team: Søren Ahrendt, Anders Danø, Abbas Fathi, Kim Franke, Peter
Houd, Mikael Knudsen, Trine Majgaard, Jette Sandberg, Morten
Vedelsbøl
Awards: MIPIM Award 2016 (finalist), Arkitekturprisen Aabenraa
Kommune 2016 (commendation), European Healthcare Design Awards
2016 (finalist in Best Healthcare Development), International Academy
for Design and Health Awards 2017 (category Mental Health Design)

Östra Hospital Emergency Psychiatry Ward
Location: Gothenburg, Sweden
Status: Completed 2006
Client: Västfastigheter
Lead architect: Maria Wetter Öhman
Team: Stefan Lundin, Krister Nilsson, Stig Olsson, Elisabeth Rosenlund,
Elisabeth Sandberg, Maria Wetter Öhman
Awards: Forum's Healthcare Building Award 2007, WAN Healthcare
Building of the Year Award 2009 (finalist)

Forensic Psychiatry with a Human Face
Researcher: Stefan Lundin, ARQ research project 2015

Status: Published 2017
Report title: Rågården – Rättspsykiatri med mänskligt ansikte. Eds.
Claes Caldenby, Stefan Lundin, ARQ Gothenburg 2017
Research team/co-authors: Claes Caldenby, Frances Hagelbäck
Hansson, Elsa Ivarson, Stefan Lundin, Lennart Ring

Hóspital Simón Bolívar
Location: Bogotá, Colombia
Status: Design proposal 2015
Client: Nordic Investment Bank/Swedish Ministry for Foreign Affairs
Lead architect: Cristiana Caira
Team: Björn Bondesson, Cristiana Caira, Joel Hördin, Saga Karlsson,
Bruno Manrique Carrera, Carl Mölander, Elin Rittmark

Radiation Therapy Centre
Location: Lund, Sweden
Status: Completed 2013
Client: RegionService
Lead architect: Lena Brand
Team: Ia Belfrage, Per Berg, Lena Brand, Ulrika Connheim, Peter
Eklund, Abbas Fathi, Annelie Håkansson, Helena Hirvonen, Anna- Karin
Jägare, Birgit Löfkvist, Markus Magnusson, Marthe Myrvoll,
Kjell Nyberg, Katarina Rasmusson, Martin Vozzi, Anneli Wihlborg
Awards: Lunds Stadsbyggnadspris 2013 (Urban Planning Award)

Hocus Focus: Creating a brighter hospital experience
Researchers: Johanna Augustsson (interior architect), Mikaela Åström
Forsgren (lighting designer), White Research Lab 2014
Report title: Hokus Fokus
Location: Queen Silvia's Children's Hospital, Gothenburg, Sweden
Status: Completed 2016
Client: Insamlingsstiftelsen för Drottning Silvias barn- och
ungdomssjukhus

Linköping University Hospital
Location: Linköping, Sweden
Status: Completed 2016
Client: Östergötland County Council, FM-centrum
Lead architects: Linda Mattsson, Eva Berg
Team: Renato Adriasola Orellana, Eva Berg, Francesca Bianchi, Helen
Biddle, Karl Brodefors, Åsa Carlestam, Anders Ekberg, Anna Graaf,
Marie-Louise Greger, Alexander Hägg, Henric Hammarslätt, Fredrik
Hennings, Annika Jägevall, Susanne Klämfeldt, Agnete Klinkby Jensen,
Ola Lindblad, Anna-Karin Lisell Selling, Cuong Ly, Henrik Magnusson,
Linda Mattsson, Thomas Peinert, Daniel Peterson, Karin Planting-
Bergloo, Helena Polgård, Ulrika Romare, Elisabeth Rosenlund, Rebecca
Rubin, Gustav Söderberg Röstlund, Emma Stridh, Gith Thellsén, Pilvi
Vanamo, Caroline Varnauskas, Barbara Vogt, Caroline Werner, Lena
Zetterberg
Environmental certification: Miljöbyggnad Silver (Environmental Design
Level Silver)

House of Heroes
Location: Umeå, Sweden
Status: Completed 2017
Client: Västerbottens County Council/Föreningen Hjältarnas hus
Lead architect: Lennart Sjögren
Team: Katharina Björlin Wiklund, Egil Blom, Anna-Carin Dahlberg,
Roger Edvinsson, Katrin Ehnberg-Gunnarsson, Daniel Hultman, Mattias
Lind, Jens Lindh, Kjell Nyberg, Lennart Sjögren
Environmental certification: Miljöbyggnad Guld (Environmental Design
Level Gold): certification pending

New Mother and Child Unit, Panzi Hospital
Location: Bukavu, Democratic Republic of Congo
Status: Design proposal 2017

ARQ Research Project: report 2017 by research team Cristiana Caira,
Maria Glädt, Tania Sande Beiro
Client: Panzi Hospital
Lead architect: Cristiana Caira
Team: Cristiana Caira, Magnus Carlstrand, Maria Glädt, Saga Karlsson,
Johan Lundin, Carl Molin, Agnes Orstadius, Tania Sande Beiro
In collaboration with: CSR project including Panzi Hospital, The Centre
for Healthcare Architecture (CVA) at Chalmers University, WSP,
University of Gothenburg and Art of Life and Birth

New Karolinska Solna
Location: Solna, Sweden
Status: Completed 2017
Client: Stockholms Läns Landsting. OPS partner: Scandinavian
Hospital Partner (SHP)
Architects: White Tengbom Team, including Arkitema/DOT, Reflex,
Respons
Lead architects: Per-Mats Nilsson (CEO White Tengbom Team),
Hans Forsmark (White), Tomas Boijsen (Tengbom)
Team: White Tengbom Team
Environmental certification: LEED Gold, Miljöbyggnad Guld
(Environmental Design Level Gold)
Awards: European Healthcare Design Awards: Future Healthcare
Design category 2017

Hygienic Handle: Reducing bacterial transfer by design
Researcher/designer: Jörgen Pell, White Research Lab 2014
Location: Karolinska University Hospital Solna
Status: Design implemented at Karolinska University Hospital
Solna 2016
Report title: Hygienic Handle – Sjukhusanpassat trycke,
JÖAP Design
Research collaboration: Hans Forsmark (White), Andreas Sture (White),
Mats Holmberg (White), Anders Birgersson (Assa Abloy)

Carlanderska Hospital
Location: Gothenburg, Sweden
Status: Completed 2017
Lead architect: Ulla Antonsson
Team: Ulla Antonsson, Elin Hultman, Roger Johansson,
Krister Nilsson, Fabian Sahlqvist, Lars Zackrisson

Picture Credits

People

Wanawsha Abdullah

Valny Adalsteinsdottir

Tarek Adhami

Renato Adriasola Orellana

Hamia Aghaiemeybodi

Ivan Agoes

Aleksander Ågren

Anna Ågren

Jimmie Ahlgren

Jonatan Ahlmark

Hanna Ahlström Isacson

Søren Ahrendt

Anders Åkeflo

Agnes Åkerblad

Kristina Åkerlund

Tobias Åkerlund

Alexander Åkerman

Angelica Åkerman

Sheraz Al Hasan

Malin Alenius

Andreas Alexandersson

Oskar Allerby

Joakim Allerth

Anton Almqvist

Mahmoud al-Shihabi

Ioannis Anagnostopoulos

Frans Andersen

Jonathan Anderson

Marcus Anderson

Annika Andersson

Christer Andersson

Jens Rasmus Andersson

Per-Anders Andersson

Rickard Andersson

Robin Andersson

Sara Andersson

Tony Andersson

Nadja Andilėr

Pär Andréasson

Stephanie Angeraini

Fredrik Angner

Pål Annerström

Oskar Anselmsson

Ulla Antonsson

Jan Anundi

Marios Aphram

Fredrik Arbell

Anders Arfvidsson

Anna Arias

Tomas Aronsson

Åsa Askergren

Daniel Asp

Edvin Asteberg

Lars Åstrand

Mikaela Åström Forsgren

Matilda Åström

Johanna Augustsson

Maria Aurell

Jens Axelsson

Per Axenborg

Arya Azadrad

Ingrid Backman

Johan Backman

Carl Bäckstrand

Mehdi Bahrami

Nicholas Baker

Gunvor Bakke Kvinlog

Kristjan Baldvinsson

Angeliki Baltoyianni

Gabriela Banic Hjörvar

Helda Bara

Saina Barazande

Louise Bården

Anna Barne

Luis Barri

Sara Barton

Gina Bast Mossige

Ia Belfrage

Malin Belfrage

Jonathan Bell

Cecilia Bengtsson

Heléne Bengtsson

Michelle Bengtsson

Jerome Beresford

Ulrika Bergbrant

Gunilla Berggren

Vera Berggren

Marlene Bergqvist

Eleanor Bergren

Ulla Bergström

Anna Berlin

Anna Bernmark

Francesca Bianchi

Helen Biddle

Angelica Bierfeldt Liptak

Nicola Bigmore

Åsa Bjerndell

Johan Björkholm

Dan Björklund

Katharina Björlin Wiklund

Linda Björling

Karin Björning-Engström

Drenusha Blakcori

Sarah Blake Elmvall

Bo Blixt

Elena Bloch

Paula Block Philipsen

Egil Blom

Natalie Blom

Anders Bobert

Marta Bohlmark

Freya Bolton

Björn Bondesson

Tove Bonnedal

David Bonsib

Simon Borg

Viktor Borg

Anja Borges

Magnus Borglund

Fredrik Borgström

Nina Borgström

Ingemar Börjesson

Mette Boye

Lena Brand

Yaël Bratel

Ulf Brattö

Victoria Brodefors

Patrik Buchinger

Magnus Bunner

Viktoria Buskqvist

Emma Butler

Jialu Cai

Cristiana Caira

Arthur Campling

Gisela Carlén

Åsa Carlestam

Birgitta Carlsson

Marta Casagrande

Lucas Cedergren

Caroline Cederström

Havar Cemal

Maeva Chardon

Marcus Chiu

Navid Christensen

Solvejg Christensen

Dennis Christiansen

Anna Christoffersson

David Christoffersson

Gabriel Ciardi

Thomas Claesson

Martin Clase

Susanne Clase

Fredrik Collin

Raluca-Maria Constantinescu

Filiz Coskun

Rafel Crespo Solana

Magnus Croon

Masara Dagdony

Anna-Carin Dahlberg

Johan Dahlberg

Ellen Dahlgren

Helena Dahlgren

Sarah Dahman Meyersson

Ina Dalsgaard Gouliaev

Jakob Danckwardt-Lillieström

Anders Danø

Clara Daoud

Eva Datta

Charlotta Davidsson

Lina Davidsson

Andrew Davies

Bryn Davies

Simone de Bergh

Niels de Bruin

Emma Deines

Ola Dellson

Geoff Denton

Adalaura Diaz Garcia

Louise Didriksson

Carl Dolk

Emelie Doverbo

Marie-Claude Dubois

Sanam Ebadnejad

Pia Eckerstein

Anna Edblom

Sofia Edholm

John Philip Edstrand

Roger Edvinsson

Patrik Edwardh

August Edwards

Mats Egelius

Anna Egerbo

Andreas Eggertsen Teder

Martin Ehn Hillberg

Katrin Ehnberg-Gunnarsson

Ingrid Ehrnebo

Anna Maria Ejdeholm

Lars-Magnus Ejdeholm

Anders Ejdeholt

Frida Ejdemyr

Marie-Louise Ejlev

Ann-Sofie Ek

Linda Ekblom

Pi Ekblom

Charlotta Ekelund Ingvar

Maria Ekenberg

Anna Ekholm

Anna Eklund

Claes Eklund

Heidi Eklund

Linda Ekman

Susanna Elewi

Anna-Lena Elfving

Mirwais Elham

Julia Eliasson

Martina Eliasson

Torbjörn Eliasson

Thérèse Elmquist

Malin Elvestad

Lena Enebjörk

Ulla Enetjärn

Dan Engberg

Johanna Engberg

Malin Ericson

Linda Ericsson

Erik Eriksson

Frida Eriksson

Helene Eriksson

Krister Eriksson

Martin Eriksson

Mattias Eriksson

Niklas Eriksson

Päivi Eriksson

Therese Eriksson

Raquel Eriksson Elep

Mia Erlandsson

Amanda Ersson

Ulrika Essner

Eva Fabricius

Erik Falkenström

Dermot Farrelly

Mike Fedak

Fredrik Fernek

Thiago Ferreira

Hanne Finseth

Caitlin Fitzgerald

Jake Ford

Gustav Fornwall

Hanna-Clara Forsberg

Malin Forsberg

Stefan Forsberg

Tobias Forsgren

Hans Forsmark

Rasmus Forster

Clara Fraenkel

Kim Franke

Hugo Franklin

Lisa Fransson

Linus Fransson von Essen

Charlotte Fredholm

Maria Fredriksson

Niclas Frenning

Catrin Frid

Andreas Fridh

Teodor Fridman

Morten Frisch

Amanda Fröler

Klara Frosterud

János Fuchs

Magnus Gabrielsson

Felipe Garcia

Lars Garrit

Jonathan Gertson

Nazdar Ghalali

Ali Ghorbanamraji

Silja Glomb

Maria Glädt

Gusten Göthe

Viktor Göthe

Anna Graaf

Sara Grahn

Mikaela Grassl

Scott Grbavac

Ola Grimell

Matteo Grometto

Daniel Groop

Elise Grosse

Annika Grottell

Gunilla Grönbeck

Elin Grönberg

Louise Grönberg

Petra Grönqvist

Sven Gunnarson

Frida Gustafson

Johan Gustafsson

Josefin Gustafsson

Olle Gustafsson

Sven Gustafsson

Olov Gynt

Lina Gustafsson Moberg

Ulrika Håård

Elin Haettner

Gunilla Hagberg

Alexandra Hagen

Carl Hägerström

Alexander Hägg

Thyra Häggstam

Marie Håkansson

Johanna Hallgren

Charlotta Hallström

Elsa Hallström

Elin Hammarsten

Gunilla Hansson

Jens Hansson

Joakim Hansson

Hugo Hardell

Sofie Hardmark

Åsa Haremst

Karin Hartmann
Marie Havard-Delcey
Erik Hedborg
Karin Hedén
Anna Hedlund
Karin Hedlund
Fredrik Hedvall
Joel Heinevik
Monika Hellekant
Anna Hellsing
Charlotta Hellström
Josefin Hellström Olson
John Helmfridsson
Alexander Henriksson
Emma Herbert
Maria Hermansson
Victor Hugo Hernandez Talavera
Tobias Hesselgren
Marcus Heverius
Anna Hidemark
Gunnar Hidemark
Carina Hillerö
Stina Hillinge
Elin Hirsch
Helena Hirvonen
Edda Hjörvar
Bo Hofsten
Örjan Högberg
Maria Höier
Anja Hole
Timon Holgers
Heidi Holm Jensen
Birgitte Holm
Alexandra Holman
Mathias Holmberg
Sanna Holmberg
Britta Holmblad
Albin Holmgren
Johan Holmgren
Maria Hörberg
Karin Höök
Joel Hördin
Yara Hormazábal Cortés
Marty Hughes
Maria Hult
Agnete Hultberg
Jonas Hultgren
Daniel Hultman
Elin Hultman
Rikard Hultman
Katrine Hvidt
Jonna Idsäter
Noor Ismail

Andreas Ivarsson
Sander Izikowitz
Anton Jakobsson
Karin Jakobsson
Erik Järinge
Anna Jarkiewicz
Cecilia Jarlöv
Gustav Jarlöv
Susan Jayne Carruth
Birgit Jensen
Søren Jeppe Sørensen
Johanna Jerremalm
Åke Johansson
Alexander Johansson
Björn Johansson
David Johansson
Jenny Johansson
Leif Johansson
Maria Johansson
Mats Johansson
Roger Johansson
Sanna Johnels
Douglas Johnson
Jack Johnson
Martin Johnson
Peter Johnstone
Lisa Jonas
Annika Jonasson
Thomas Jonasson
Mia Jonson
Caroline Jönsson
Kristofer Jonsson
Raimo Joss
Joel Jouannet
Jasmina Jovanovic Holm
Aksel Alvarez Jurgueson
Elise Juusela-Norberg
Mark Kaiser
Jesper Källgren
Fredrik Källström
Elena Kanevsky
Fotis Kapaniris
Camilla Kappel
Yara Karkouh
Anna Karlsson
Filippa Karlsson
Kristin Karlsson
Saga Karlsson
Maud Karlström
Jessica Kaspersen
Cagil Kayan Widegren
Anna Kerr
Sam Keshavarz

Tze Hui Khor
Fredric Kihlberg
Lovisa Kihlborg
Erik Kiltorp
Young Ill Kim
Gunnar Kjellerstedt
Susanne Klämfeldt
Anna-Johanna Klasander
Bo Kleberger
Simon Klejs Gren
Agnete Klinkby Jensen
Mikael Knudsen
Magdalena Koistinen
Carin Kollberg
Elvira Koman
Taiga Koponen
Jessica Kos
Stelios Kostakis
Jozefin Kraft
Koen Kragting
Marie Pia Kristiansen
Anna Krook
Katarina Krupinska
Nils Krus
Jessica Kusnadi
Jonas Kvant

Maria Laakso
Claudia Laarmann
Lisa Läckgren
Maria Lagging
Emir Lamti
Thomas Landenberg
Tomas Landfeldt
Karl Landin
Ylva Langeby
Håkan Langseth
Karin Lantz
Dan Larsson
Fredrik Larsson
Ida Larsson
Jan Larsson
Måns Larsson
Mikael Larsson
Lise-Lott Larsson Kolessar
Kasra Lashkari
Stig Lassen
Raphael Le Gall
Inge-Lise Leander
Karin Leckström
Lisa Lee Källman
Rebecca Leissner
Annie Leonsson

Peter Leuchovius
Sofia Lewén
Yupeng Lian
Oskar Lierud
Katarina Liljeberg
Anna Liljekvist
Kristoffer Lind
Mattias Lind
Erik Lindahl
Andreea Lindberg
Martin Lindberg
Ola Lindblad
Hanna Linde
Carl Lindecrantz
Caroline Lindgård
Magnus Lindgren
Jens Lindh
Sofia Lindhoff
Henrik Lindholm
Teresa Lindholm
Oskar Lindqvist
Krister Lindstedt
Karl Lindstrand
Elin Lindström
Malin Lindström
Moa Lindunger
Jonas Lindvall
Erik Linn
Fanny Linnros
Moa Lipschütz
Anna-Karin Lisell Selling
Daniel Lisskar
Ellen Lock
Magnus Löfvendahl
Morten Lolk
Sine Lolk Andersen
Siri Lönnroth Himmelman
Mikael Lorensson
Graciela Loscalzo
Jesper Løve Nielsen
Magdalena Lund
Camilla Lundell
Erik Lundgren
Marja Lundgren
Moa Lundholm
Johan Lundin
Karin Lundin
Stefan Lundin
Jakob Lundkvist
Jacob Lundqvist
Kajsa Lundqvist
Lotten Lundqvist
Marie Lundqvist

Cuong Ly
Camilla Lystrand
Lisa Läckgren
Paula Mackenzie
Anton Magnusson
Erik Magnusson
Frans Magnusson
Henrik Magnusson
Markus Magnusson
Niels Majgaard
Robert Makdisi
Jenny Mäki
Arvid Malm
Kenneth Malmqvist
Malin Malmqvist
Katja Manninen
Bruno Manrique Carrera
Mari-Liis Männik
Matilda Månsdotter
Alexandra Manson
Viktor Martinsson
Rikard Matson
Linda Mattsson
Anders Medin
Anika Meincke
Joan Melgaard Rasmussen
Jacob Melin
Lisa Melin
Viktor Melin
Lina Melki
Helena Mellberg
Karolina Mellberg
Samuel Michaëlsson
Ronny Millegård
Andreas Milsta
Nina Minjevic
Andreas Mitsiou
Silke Modes
Hanna Modin
Jens Modin
Carl Molin
Anna Montgomery
Asbjörn Morsing Thomasen
Frida Munktell
Marthe Myrvoll
Maria Navarro
Magnus Nellström
Ingela Nevbäck
Jens Niehues
Annette Nielsen
Bjørn K. Nielsen
Ann Nilsson
Anna Nilsson

Daniel Nilsson
Fredrik G. Nilsson
Fredrik Mats Nilsson
Jacob Nilsson
Jonas Nilsson
Karolina Nilsson
Katarina Nilsson
Krister Nilsson
Lars Nilsson
Lars-Erik Nilsson
Lillemor Nilsson
Margaretha Nilsson
Maria Nilsson
Mathias Nilsson
Mattias Nilsson
Peter Nilsson
Sofi Nilsson
Ulrika Nilsson
Viktor Nilsson
Robert Niziolek
Dirk Noack
Ulrika Nobelius
Marte Noedtvedt Skjaeggestad
Nilserik Norberg
Olof Nordenson
Jenny Nordius Stålhamre
Anna Nordlander
John Nordmark
Oskar Nordquist
Linn Nordström
Mattias Nordström
Stina Nordström
Oskar Norelius
Björn Norén
Terese Norén
Emma Norlén
Josefin Norén Almén
Malin Norling
Mikael Norman
Stina Norman
Karin Nyberg
Kjell Nyberg
Mona Nygård Jørgensen
Erik Nygren
Inga Nygren
Rickard Nygren
Jonathan Nyman
Ylva Nyren
Maria Nyström
Milla Nyström
Nadja Odenhage
Anna Öhlin
Rikard Ohlson

Sandra Ohlsson	Kristina Philipson	Jonatan Sahlin
Anders Olausson	Zlatko Pilipovic	Fabian Sahlqvist
Elisabeth Olausson	Hanna Plato	Jacob Sahlqvist
Lucia Olavarri Casado	Pernille Ploug Sølby	Kinna Sahlqvist
Linda Oldhage Peterson	Helena Polgård	Sophie Sahlqvist
Marie Olofsson	Joseph Price	Sara Sako
Sten M. Olsen	Nilda Pulga	Johanna Salomonsson
Cecilia Olson	Poul Raahauge	Anna-Karin Salovaara
August Olsson	Sigrid Raaschou-Nielsen	Magnus Samuelsson-Gamboa
Bo-Magnus Olsson	Therese Radeklev	Åsa Sandberg
Håkan Olsson	Johanna Raflund Tobisson	Elisabeth Sandberg
Kristina Olsson	Ingmar Rahm	Tania Sande Beiro
Lars Olsson	Johanna Rand	Julia Sandgren
Lovisa Olsson	Shilan Rasha	Elin Sandström
Maria Olsson	Charlotta Råsmark	Jan Sandström
Per Olsson	Donna Rasmussen	Ingjerd Sandven Kleivan
Stig Olsson	Katarina Rasmusson	Nora Sarii
Zebastian Olsson	James Reader	Mattia Scarpellino
Vladimir Ondejcik	Evelina Regenius Jouper	Rebekah Schaberg
Ellen Ordell	Eric Reid	Liselott Schantz
Lena Orrberg	Tatu Rekola	Lars B. Schmidt
Agnes Orstadius	Agne Revellé	Robert Schmitz
Maria Orvesten	Ann-Marie Revellé	Bjørn Schølardt
Oliver Osborne	Linda Ringqvist	Elisabeth Schrotti
Lena Osvalds	Carolina Ritz	Sander Schuur
Peter Øxnæs	Giovanni Rodi	Monika Semkowicz
Libny Pacheco	Anna Röjdeby	Solveig Sennerholm
Alejandro Pacheco Diéguez	Ana Romano	Maha Shalaby
Karin Palm	Nagler Maria Romano Barbosa	Maryam Shojai
Sofia Palmer	Ulrika Romare	Catharina Siegbahn
Rafael Palomo	Malin Romo	Jenny Siira
Martin Pålsson	Lisa Rönnols	Niklas Singstedt
Anders Parment	Elin Rooth	Felix Sjöberg
Alan Paterson	Maria Ros	Josef Sjöberg
Julia Patey	Charlotta Rosell	Rikard Sjöberg
Malin Paulsson	Carl Magnus Rosén	Viktor Sjöberg
Thomas Peinert	Tommy Rosenlöf	Fabian Sjöblom
Aylin Pektas	Elisabeth Rosenlund	Lennart Sjögren
Jörgen Pell	Henrik Rosenqvist	Anna-Sofia Sjööquist
Marie Pell	Mathias Roth	Felicia Sjösten Harlin
Victoria Percovich Gutierrez	Steven Rowland	Frida Skantze
Jan Perotti	Kristoffer Roxbergh	Gustav Skarin
Elin Persson	Charlotte Ruben	Therese Skevik
Emma Persson	Rebecca Rubin	Erik Skytte
Fredrik Persson	Thomas Rudin	Camilla Smedéus
Johan Persson	Stefan Rummel	Michael Smith
Johanna Persson	Jonas Runberger	Annie Söder
Sofia Persson	Marianne Rutberg	Josefina Söderberg
Fredrik Petersson	Johan Rydell	Marie Söderberg
Peter Petersson	Anna Ryf	Gustav Söderberg Röstlund
Marios Petrongonas	Helena Ryhle	Åsa Söderhielm
Jenny Pettersson	Antony Saade	Marianne Söderstedt
Alison Petty	David Saand	Maria Sondén

Martina Sovré
Ulla Spaak
Kajsa Sperling
Magdalena Stål
Ellika Stare
Margaret Steiner
Marie-France Stendahl
Monika Stenholm
Ulrika Stenkula
Lasse Stenman
Daniel Stenqvist
Anna Sterner
Karin Sterner
Pontus Stigeborn
Anni Stockeld
Viktor Stoltz
Gunnar Stomrud
Ola Strandell
Filip Strebeyko
Andreas Sture
Filip Sudolsky
Christoffer Sundberg
Martin Sundberg
Lotta Sundell
IngaKarin Sundqvist
Ivar Suneson
Samantha Suppiah
Ann-Christine Svahlstedt
Johan Svartnäs
Jonas Svedäng
Pernilla Svedberg
Linda Svensson
Niklas Svensson
Simon Svensson
Sandra Sydbom
Lena Sylwan
Hans Tang
Erik Ternstedt
Mikkel Thams Olsen
Gith Thellsén
Linda Thiel
Freya Tigerschiöld
Sofia Tillberg
Johan Torarp
Jenny Tordrup
Karin Törnquist
Malin Törnqvist
Elsa Törnros
Kjell Torstensson
Erik Torvén
Theodor Tsesmatzoglou
Rita Tuorila
Anders Tväråna

Anna Uhlin
Roger van Bergen
Raymond van der Heijden
Kaveh Vaez
Mette Vangkilde
Caroline Varnauskas
Joachim Vemmerstad
Emil Vest Hansen
Björn Vestlund
Christina Vildinge
Jónatan Virgala López
Linda Vodopija Stark
Barbara Vogt
Susanna von Eyben
Anna von Gegerfelt
Ann-Britt von Schedvin
Monica von Schmalensee
Martin Vozzi
Pia Wacker
Cecilia Waern
Sofia Waernulf
Mats Wåhlin
Johan Wahlqvist
Christian Wahlström
Charlotta Wallander
Henrik Wallander
Viktoria Walldin
Christian Wallenborg
Ulrika Wallin
Tom Waltilla
Victoria Wang
Anna Weber
Sofie Weidemann
Mikael Welander
Lennart Wennström
Petter Wesslander
Emelie Westergren
Mirja Westling
Fredrik Westlund
Josef Wiberg
Helena Wickholm
Oskar Widlund
Göran Wihl
Anders Wiil
Rebecka Wijk
Jan Wijkmark
Per Wikfeldt
Josefine Wikholm
Nils Arvid Wiking
Monica Wild
Jay Williams
Lisa Wistrand
Nina Wittlöv Löfving

Andrew Worsley
Cecilia Wretlind
Anna Wretlind el-Sayed
Laura Nicoline Wulffsberg
Annika Yledahl
Sara Yllner
Tianle Yu
Maja Zachrisson
Lars Zackrisson
Malgorzata Zboinska
Ania Zdunek
Dag Zerne
Anna Zimdahl
Malin Zimm
Max Zinnecker